JN255695

THE
South Indian
Vegetarian Kitchen

はじめてのベジタリアン南インド料理

Hema Parekh

ヘーマ・パレック

Dedication

To

my parents Lalchand and Nila Gandhi
and
my children Ayesha and Alok

AMBASSADOR OF INDIA
भारत का राजदूत

<u>MESSAGE</u>

I am happy to learn that Ms. Hema Parekh, an active member of the Indian community, is publishing her fourth book, this time focusing on South Indian vegetarian recipes.

Indian cuisine has gained tremendous popularity across Japan in recent years, with the Indian curry offering a new choice to Japanese palates that have for long enjoyed the "Japanese curry". Indian restaurants are now ubiquitous in Tokyo and in major cities.

Ms. Hema Parekh has long experience in promoting Indian cuisine in Japan. She has earlier published two books in Japanese on vegetarian Indian cuisine, in addition to a book in English titled "Asian Vegan Kitchen".

In her new book, Ms. Hema Parekh has painstakingly researched each recipe and subjected it to rigorous verification. The broad range of South Indian vegetarian food covered in this book is an invaluable addition to the nascent vegetarian repertoire available in Japan. With the help of this book, many more in Japan will be able to savour the gastronomic delights of authentic South Indian cuisine.

Ms. Hema Parekh's book is being published in 2017, which has been jointly declared by the Prime Ministers of India and Japan as the Year of Friendly Exchanges. I offer Ms. Hema Parekh my congratulations and I hope that this book will bring the joys of South Indian cooking to every home in Japan.

Tokyo
19 April 2017

(**Sujan R. Chinoy**)

在日インド人のコミュニティーでご活躍されているヘーマ・パレック氏が、4冊目の著書・南インドのベジタリアン料理本を出版されるとお聞きし、大変嬉しく思います。

近年、インド料理店は、東京をはじめあらゆる場所にあることからも、日本中で人気を博しています。長年"日本式のカレー"を楽しんできた日本人の味覚に、インドカレーは新たな選択肢となることと存じます。

ヘーマ・パレック氏は日本でインド料理を促進してこられた長い経験をお持ちです。『Asian Vegan Kitchen』という英語版の著書の他に、2冊のベジタリアン料理本を出版されています。

一つ一つのレシピを入念に研究し、厳密に検証されていることからも、この本で網羅されている南インドのベジタリアン料理の幅広いメニューは、日本で広まりつつあるベジタリアン料理のレパートリーに、とても貴重なメニューを加えることになります。この本をきっかけに、日本のより多くの方々に、本格的な南インド料理の美食の品々をご賞味いただけることでしょう。

ヘーマ・パレック氏の新刊は、印日の両首相によって、友好交流の年として連名で宣言された2017年に出版されます。

ヘーマ・パレック氏にお祝いを申し上げますとともに、この本が南インド料理の喜びを、日本の各ご家庭にもたらすことを願っています。

2017年4月19日 東京

在日インド大使 スジャンR・チノイ

Contents
目次

Column コラム

Curry and Soup
カレー & スープ

Rice and Noodle
ライス & ヌードル

My Story

マイストーリー

私は、南インドの都市チェンナイ（当時はマドラスという名前の地）で生まれました。生後2～3ヵ月のとき、両親と共にムンバイに移り住みましたが、南インドは、私にとって永遠に、人生の旅の一部として残る地です。

私のインスピレーションの源は、父と母にあります。どんなときでも、二人に誇りに思ってもらえるように努めています。

ムンバイでの幼少期は、楽しい学生生活を送りました。放課後は近所の子供たちと遊んで過ごしたり、週末は妹と弟たちと海の中を歩いたり、ビーチで貝殻を見つけたり。中でも一番好きな思い出は、家族とインドの色々な場所を旅行した休日の思い出です。携帯電話やパソコン、テレビさえもなかった時代は、素朴な楽しみがありました。両親が山のように本を持って帰ってくれたり、友人や親戚が遊びに来てくれたときは、とても幸福を感じる時間でした。

私と主人が出会ったのは、大学3年のときでした。すぐに婚約をし、大学4年になる前に結婚をしました。大急ぎで一人前になる準備をし、主人が仕事を始める日本へ移り住むことになりました。

私が乗った飛行機が東京に到着した日は、1980年1月の寒い夜のこと。空から雪が降っていたのを覚えています。辺り一面は、見渡す限りのやわらかい毛布のような雪。新しい場所で新しい人生をスタートすることは、純粋で幸先のよいことのようでした――。ところが、東京で野菜や果物の値段を見てショックを受けました。8本入りのオクラ一袋の値段が、80インドルピー相当（インドでオクラ1キロが買える金額）だったのです! さらに現実を突きつけられたのは、当時私がまったく料理ができなかったことです。「ポテトカレーに何のスパイスを使うべきか?」と、母に何度も電話をかけ尋ねるほどでした。次の帰省の際には、キッチンに張りつき母のテクニック一つ一つを覚える努力をしました。母が食べ物にスパイスやハーブを気軽に投入する姿、料理へのその柔軟な姿勢こそが、美味しい料理の秘訣なのだと気がつきました。そうして得た学びは、"レシピ通りに調理するのではなく、使用する材料の感覚を高めることが大切なのだ"ということでした。本来、インド料理はすべての人にとって、柔軟で、自由で、楽しい体験になるものですから。この気づきをきっかけに、私の料理に対する興味は、境地を開くことになりました。

子供たちが東京のインターナショナルスクールに通っていたこともあり、私のまわりには、友人をはじめ、世界中から来た素晴らしい沢山の先生がいました。私は彼らから独自の家庭料理を教わり、それを自分のキッチンで再現することを試みました。インドの友人たちの間では、異なる地域から来た人たちが多く、それぞれの地方の料理を知ることができました。子供たちが小さい頃方々に旅をしたときは、行った先々で郷土料理についての知識を教えてくださる興味深い方々と巡り合いました。

私たちは家を開放し、子供たちの友人がいつ来ても食事を振る舞えるよう歓迎をしました。食べ物を美味しそうにほおばる彼らの笑顔は、新しい料理を試し続ける励みとなったのです。また、主人と私の友人のおもてなしをしてきた中で、私の料理は賛辞をいただくことができました。フレッシュな野菜や材料で作った料理を、家族や友人が喜んでくれたことは、私の幸せとなりました。

日本で料理のレッスンを始めてから、25年以上が経ちます。様々な国から来ている生徒の皆さんや日本の生徒の皆さんは、楽しいおしゃべりと笑いとともに、いろいろな意味で私の人生を豊かにしてくれています。

私が料理をはじめた頃は、ここまで料理を愛し職業にまでするとは、決して想像もしていませんでした。気がつけば、日本にきてから約30年。世界の料理を研究してきた私の道のりは、本当に価値あるものになりました。

私の物語は、娘のアイーシャと息子のアロックを語ることなしでは完結しません。彼らは長い間に渡り、私のそばにいてインスピレーションをあたえてくれただけでなく、心の支えとなり私の創造力に火をつけてくれる存在です。

前作の『The Asian Vegan Kitchen』では、私は9ヵ国を旅しました。そして今、"南インドへの旅"を綴っています。この本を手にとった皆さんが、同じようにこの旅をご堪能くださることを願っています。

I was born in Chennai, when it was still called Madras. And although I was barely a few months old, when I moved with my parents to Mumbai, the region will remain a part of my life journey forever.

My mother and my father are my inspiration and to this day, I strive to make them proud in everything I do.

My childhood in Mumbai is full of happy memories. Fun school days, and evenings spent playing in the building compound with the neighborhood kids. I remember weekend mornings spent at the beach with my brother and sisters, wading in the sea, and looking for sea shells.

Some of my fondest memories are of family holidays to different parts of India. With no smartphones, computers, or even color TV, life was about simple pleasures. We would be overjoyed when our parents brought home a stash of books to read, or when friends and relatives came over.

I was in my third year of college when I met my husband at a family gathering. We were soon engaged, and married by my senior year. I had to grow up quickly, and was soon on my way to Japan, where my husband was starting his business. It was a cold January night in 1980 when our flight landed in Tokyo. I remember seeing snowflakes falling out of the sky. There was a soft blanket of snow as far as I could see. It seemed like a pure, auspicious way to start a new life, in a new place – or so I thought.

I was in shock when I saw the prices of fruits and vegetables in Tokyo. One pack of okra, with 8 pieces cost the equivalent of INR 80, which would have gotten me 1kg of okra back home. Then came another realization, I couldn't cook at all. Frantic calls were made to my mother, asking whether I should use mustard seeds or cumin seeds in a potato curry.

On my next trip home I was glued to the kitchen, watching everything my mother did and trying to memorize the techniques. The ease with which she threw the spices and herbs into food was fascinating, and in that attitude, lay the secret.

My first real lesson was that cooking delicious food isn't about getting the recipe just right. It's about developing a feel for the ingredients and the right quantities. There is an inherent flexibility in Indian cooking which makes it a liberating experience for all.

Back in Tokyo, my interest in cooking soon led me to expand my culinary boundaries. With two children attending international schools in Tokyo, I was surrounded by wonderful people from all over the world. I found many new teachers in my friends, who taught me their style of home cooking, which I tried to recreate in my own kitchen.

We travelled extensively around the world, while the children were young and everywhere we went, I came across interesting people who shared their knowledge about the local cuisine.

Ours was an open home, where my children's friends were always welcome and had a meal waiting for them, no matter what time they walked in. The smile on their faces, as they scarfed down plates of food was all the encouragement I needed to keep trying new dishes.

My husband and I are fortunate to have many friends, and over the years, we have entertained family and friends from all over the world, in our Tokyo home. In the early years, receiving compliments on my cooking was very encouraging.

I loved what I could do with fresh produce, and how food took shape in my hands and the joy my dishes gave to my family and friends.

Soon I began giving cooking classes, and I have been doing so for the past 25 years. My international and Japanese students have enriched my life in so many ways with the laughter and chatter that we shared.

When I first started cooking, I never imagined that it would become such a passion, and eventually my profession. My journey from a young woman who found herself unexpectedly in a foreign country to a global culinary explorer of sorts, has been a fascinating one.

My story would not be complete without the mention of my children, Ayesha and Alok. Together, they have been a constant source of inspiration, strength and support to me.

In my most recent book, The Asian Vegan Kitchen, we took a journey through nine different countries. This time, I hope you enjoy delving into the rich cuisine of South India as much as I have enjoyed bringing it to you.

Introduction

はじめに

インドは神秘的な国です。その文化・伝統・民族・言語・色彩・音、そして「食べ物」が、最も重要なものとして位置づけられています。

インドでは、「食べ物」を『感情表現』と捉えています。古代サンスクリット語には "Atihi Devo Bhave（お客様は神様である）" という言葉があります。この意味は、客人をお迎えする温かさを表しているとともに、食べ物の真髄、すなわちお祝いや愛、おもてなしといったさまざまな場面を忠実に捉えているのです。

それぞれの地域の郷土料理は、独自のユニークな地理や歴史、文化的な語彙でかたち作られるので、上記を表現するために使われる料理法やテクニックは、インドの地域によって大きく異なります。

インド北部のパンジャブ州の食べ物は、パラク・パニールのように極彩色で風味豊かなものが特徴的。そこに住む人々や文化の活気を反映しています。インド東部のベンガル州は、ガンジス川の三角州の淡水の川を誇り、多くの種類のシーフード料理があります。ペスコ・ベジタリアン（魚も食べる菜食主義者）も多い地域です。インド西部の厳しい砂漠地帯のラジャスタン州は、ケール・サングリのような乾燥食材を使った料理を生み出しています。

そして、インド南部にはケララ州、タミルナドゥー州、カルナータカ州、アンドラ・プラデシュ州、テランガナ州という5つの革新的な州があり、連邦直轄地域ポンディチェリと共に南インドを構成していて、岩石の多い地域を除いて、南部は広い海外線。そして青々と茂った森やココナッツ林、緑の丘を誇っています。各州には独特な言語をはじめ、アイデンティティ、伝統、遺産といった文化の特徴があります。

南インドでは、主要穀物は米を中心に、ココナッツ、タマリンド、カレーリーフがふんだんに使われているほか、日常的な家庭の食事でサンバルやラッサムが出され、北インド料理とははっきりと区別されています。

修行や寺院でのクリシュナ神への奉納が、有名な菜食料理となっていきました。この本の中でも登場するドーサ、イドリ、ボンダ、バダ、バッジは、典型的なウディピの寺院でふるまわれるスナックにもなっています。

伝統的な南インド料理は、バナナの葉の上に盛りつけて出され、主食であるお米は、熱いギーをたらして出され、朝食を含め、一日のいつでも楽しまれています。

スパイスをふんだんに、かつバランスよく使用することが南インドの菜食料理の特徴です。多くの料理では、最後の技法はほとんど同じで、マスタードシード、豆、赤唐辛子とカレーリーフを組み合わせます。

本書では、南インドの名物料理はもちろん、有名な郷土料理を賛美しながら、南インドの各州のレシピをご紹介します。日本での30年以上に渡る料理家人生の中で、家族や友人たちが楽しんでくれているレシピも載せています。

ピリッと辛いサンバルやラッサムから、心が和むデザートやスイーツに至るまで、この本を通して、南インド料理の真髄を堪能していただけることでしょう。米料理をはじめ、ポリヤル、パチャディー、ワダ、チャツネ、パイサム、バターミルクドリンク、有名なフィルターコーヒー等々もご紹介します。

この本では、できるだけ南インド料理の本来の味を保ちながら、日本で手に入りやすい材料を使用しています。

ベジタリアンであるなしに関わらず、すべての読者が伝統的な南インド料理を楽しめる入門書になるようレシピを考案し、新鮮なハーブや豆、材料に重きを置き、作りやすく、料理をする皆さんが喜ぶお料理を研究しました。ビギナーをはじめ、すでに料理がお上手な方はもちろん、健康でバランスのとれた食事を風味豊かにしたいと思っている方や、友達を驚かせたいと思っている方まで、楽しみながらインド料理を味わっていただければ幸いです。

India is a magical place with a rich tapestry of interweaving cultures, traditions, people, languages, colors, sounds, and most importantly, food.

Food in India is not just a combination of ingredients and processes but an expression of emotion. 'Atithi Devo Bhava', the ancient Sanskrit phrase, meaning, 'Guest is God', describes the warmth with which a guest is welcomed into our homes and truly captures the essence of food as celebration, love, spirituality and hospitality.

The methods and techniques used to express our hospitality vary greatly throughout the country as each region's cuisine is shaped by its own unique geography, history and cultural vocabulary.

Food from the northern state of Punjab, such as Palak Paneer, is rich in color and brimming with flavor, echoing the vivacity of its people and culture. The Eastern Indian state of Bengal takes pride in their fresh water rivers in the Ganges delta, and offers large varieties of seafood. To the West, the harsh desert state of Rajasthan gave rise to cooking food from dried ingredients, such as Ker Sangri.

South India constitutes the five states of Kerala, Tamil Nadu, Karnataka, Andhra Pradesh, Telangana and the Union territory of Pondicherry. The South generally boasts a vast coastline, lush forests, coconut groves and gentle green hills. Each Southern state has its own language, identity, tradition, heritage and a distinct cultural flavor.

South Indian cuisine is distinguished from the north by a greater emphasis on rice, the liberal use of coconut, tamarind, and curry leaves and the ubiquity of sambar and rasam at all home meals. The practice of Naivedya, or religious offering to Lord Krishna at the Krishna Mutt temple in Udipi, Karnataka inspired what is known as the Udipi style of vegetarian cooking. The dosa, idli, and vada are typical Udipi snacks.

Traditionally, South Indian food is served on a banana leaf. Rice, the staple, is served with a dollop of hot liquid ghee, and enjoyed at any time of the day including breakfast. Certain rice dishes like Bisi Bela Huli Anna can be a meal by themselves.

A generous yet balanced use of spices distinguishes most of the vegetarian dishes of the region. In many dishes, the final touches remain almost the same – a careful mixture of mustard seeds, dals, dried red chilies and curry leaves.

In this book, I have introduced recipes from each of the South Indian states, celebrating renowned local dishes as well as some of the signature dishes from the region. I have also included some recipes that my family and friends have enjoyed over my 30 year-long culinary journey in Japan.

From fiery Rasams and versatile Sambars to soothing desserts and cooling drinks this book takes you through the quintessential components of a South Indian meal, including rice dishes, Poriyals, Pachadis, Vadas, Chutneys, Payasam, Masala Mor and the famous Filter Coffee,

I have used ingredients that are easy to locate in Japan, while maintaining the original essence of the dishes as much as possible.

The South Indian Vegetarian Kitchen is designed to give an introduction to traditional South Indian cuisine to all readers, vegetarian and non-vegetarian, alike. With its emphasis on fresh herbs, produce and ingredients, the recipes in the book will be easy to prepare and a delight to the palate.

Whether you are an advanced home chef and want to spice up a healthy and balanced diet, or you are just getting comfortable in the kitchen and want to surprise your friends with an exotic appetizer, there is fun to be had for everyone. A world of flavor awaits you.

Ingredients
食材紹介

── スパイス＆ハーブ ──
Spice & Herb

消化吸収、胃の働き、解毒作用などを促進します。そのまま油に入れて抽出するほか、
炒ってから粉にすれば、サラダやドリンクなどに向きます。

マスタードシード
Black Mustard Seed

独特の風味を加える小さくて黒い丸い種。南インド料理の最も重要なスパイスと言えます。チャツネや野菜料理、お米やサンバルの味を引き立たせます。

Small, round, black seeds which impart a distinct texture to a dish. A key element of South Indian cooking, mustard seeds are tempered in hot oil and used to flavor chutneys, vegetables, rice and sambar.

ターメリック
Turmeric Powder

黄色のウコンの根を粉砕して作られているインド料理に欠かせないのスパイスの1つ。免疫増強や抗酸化効果にも期待でき、その鮮やかな黄色は天然着色料としても。

One of the most essential Indian spices, turmeric powder is made by grinding its dry yellow root. This bright yellow powder is used in almost all Indian cooking. Imparts the characteristic yellow color to any dish.

アサファティーダ
Asafoetida Powder

植物の樹脂からできる、強力な香りと旨味を持つ調味料。熱い油に入れると風味がアップするので、テンパリング時に頻繁に登場します。

Also known as Hing, this strongly scented powder is a crucial ingredient which is said to add umami in Indian cooking, Asafoetida is ground and used as a powder. It has a pungent smell and is therefore used sparingly.

クミンシード
Whole Cumin Seed

インドの定番スパイスの一つ。様々な料理を風味豊かにしてくれます。ローストすると、さらに香りがアップ。料理によってシードとパウダーを使い分けます。

This quintessential Indian spice, used whole or in powdered form, is a flavorful addition to many vegetable, rice and dal dishes. Slightly larger than caraway seeds, cumin seeds have a refreshing fragrance when roasted.

クミンシードパウダー
Ground Cumin Powder

他のスパイスとミックスする際に調和するクミンシードのパウダー。料理の仕上げにかけたり、ヨーグルトをベースとしたサラダや飲み物にも使用されます。

When ground to a powder, cumin seeds integrate more fully with other seasoning ingredients. Most fragrant when freshly roasted and ground, it lends the perfect finishing touch to yogurt salads and drinks.

ブラックペッパー
Black Peppercorn

胡椒の実を乾燥させたもの。南インド料理では、ホールのまま、また砕いたりパウダーとして使用します。スナックやラッサム、野菜料理や米料理などの味つけに登場します。

Hot and spicy black peppercorns are used whole, coarsely crushed and in powdered form to enhance the flavor of snacks, rasams, vegetables and rice dishes especially in South Indian cooking.

コリアンダーシード
Coriander Seed

フレッシュなものほど薄緑色の種。焙煎すると香りが立ち、ガラムマサラ、ラッサムパウダーなどのスパイスパウダーには欠かせないスパイスです。

Plucked from the same plant as coriander leaves, the tiny, light green and hollow Coriander seeds are used both whole and in powdered form in spice mixes such as Garam Masala, Sambar and Rasam Powder.

コリアンダーパウダー
Coriander Powder

乾燥したコリアンダーの種から作られます。カレーやスナックのまろやかさと香りを出します。アジアの食品店でも購入可能です。

Also known as Dhania powder. Ground from dried coriander seeds, coriander powder is an essential spice in Indian cooking. It adds a mild flavor and aroma to curries and savory snacks.

カルダモン
Cardamom

繊細な甘さを持つ芳香性のスパイス。中に含まれる黒い種子を含め、粉砕してカルダモンパウダーとして使用されます。マサラチャイやヨーグルトドリンク、デザート。

Also known as green cardamom, this highly aromatic spice with a delicate sweetness is often used to flavor desserts, drinks and rice dishes. Each cardamom pod contains 10-12 black seeds, which are ground to make cardamom powder.

フェヌグリーグ
Fenugreek Seed

苦味が特徴の黄土色の種。焙煎すると独特の香りが生まれ、サンバルパウダーなどの調合に少量使用します。他のスパイスの風味を消してしまうので入れ過ぎに注意。

A plant with leaves and seeds which are both commonly used in Indian cooking. The small, brown and slightly bitter seeds are used sparingly in sambar and rasam, as too much of this spice can be overpowering.

サフラン
Saffron

「スパイスの女王」とも呼ばれるサフランは、世界で最も高価なスパイスです。エキゾチックな香りと特徴的な赤色が、デザートなどに使用されます。

This "Queen of Spice" ranks among the most expensive spices in the world.
Saffron is used mainly in desserts and rice dishes for its exotic flavor and characteristic red color.

フェンネルシード
Fennel Seed

八角に似た繊細な甘い香りが特徴。乾燥して焙煎したものを粉砕すると風味がよくなります。新鮮なときは緑色、時間が経つと薄い茶色に変わります。

A delicate aromatic herb which is used as a spice, fennel seeds have a sweet flavor similar to star anise. Green in color when fresh, fennel seeds are especially flavorful when dry roasted and ground.

シナモン
Cinnamon Bark

甘い香りが特徴的な、こげ茶色をしたシナモンの樹脂。スティックとパウダーがあり、料理に豊かな甘みとスパイシーな香りを加えるので、インド料理に幅広く使われています。

The aromatic dark brown bark of the cinnamon tree is widely used as a spice in Indian cooking. It is available in both stick and powder form, and imparts a rich sweet and spicy flavor.

唐辛子
Whole Dried Chilies

赤と緑、生と乾燥があり、独特の辛味を持ちます。赤い乾燥タイプの鷹の爪はテンパリングにも使用します。入れすぎに注意しましょう。

Chilies are available in various shapes and sizes, with varying degrees of intensity. Fresh chilies are hotter in taste than their dried versions. Dried red chilies are an essential ingredient in South Indian tempering.

チリパウダー
Chili Powder

2〜3種類の熟した唐辛子を乾燥・粉砕したもの。インド料理の辛さと鮮明な赤色はこのチリパウダーによるもの。産地や色によって辛さが異なります。

Made from the fruit of the pepper plant. One or more varieties of ripe red chilies are dried and ground to make chili powder. Red chili powder lends the characteristic hot taste and red color associated with Indian curries.

タマリンド
Tamarind

タマリンドは、インドやタイで広く使われているマメ科の茶色い果実。甘味料と組み合わせると甘酸っぱい味わいに。乾燥したパルプや濃縮ペーストがあります。

Known as the 'Indian date', Tamarind is the sour, brown fruit of a tropical seed pod. Widely used in South Indian and Thai cooking, it lends a beautiful sweet and sour flavor to dishes when combined with sugar. Available in dried, pulp and concentrate form.

タピオカ
Tapioca

カサバイモから採れるデンプンを加工したもの。スナックやデザートを作る際に使用されます。加熱するとゲル状の質感になり、増粘剤としても使用されることも。

A starch obtained from the cassava root. The Tapioca beads or pearls have no flavor. Generally reconstituted and used in Indian cooking to make delicious savory snacks and desserts, tapioca seeds have a gel like texture when cooked.

ココナッツパウダー／ココナッツシュレッド
Coconut Powder / Coconut Shred

南インド料理で広く使用されているココヤシの果実。カレーやスナック、野菜料理などではベースとして、またトッピングやガーニッシュとしても使用されています。

The edible nut of the coconut palm tree, is widely used in South Indian cooking. Coconut forms the base for kormas, curries and chutneys. Grated coconut is a key ingredient in many vegetable dishes, Coconut can be bought fresh, or in dried, desiccated or shredded form.

コリアンダーリーフ
Coriander Leaf

新鮮なコリアンダーの葉は、インド料理に欠かせない材料です。葉、茎、根、すべての部分が食用可能。カレーやチャツネの風味つけや、トッピングに使用されます。産地によって葉のかたちが違います。

Coriander is one of the worlds most commonly used herbs - also known as Koothmir and Clantro. It is green and leafy with a fresh citrus taste that makes it an invaluable garnish and flavor enhancer.

ベイリーフ
Bay Leaf

ローレルリーフ（月桂樹）とも呼ばれ、料理に加えることで、風味と香りをアップします。特に料理、カレー、米料理などに加えることが多いです。

Also known as laurel leaf, this long, dried leaf is used in cooking for its subtle flavor and fragrance. It enhances the aroma, especially when added to dal, curries and rice dishes.

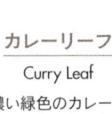

カレーリーフ
Curry Leaf

光沢のある濃い緑色のカレーリーフは香ばしさが特長で、ほとんどの南インドの料理に使われています。熱い油を加えると、魅力的な香りを放ちます。

Shiny, dark green aromatic leaves of a citrus fruit family tree. The fragrant curry leaf is a staple ingredient in South Indian cooking. It releases an enticing aroma, especially when added to hot oil in a tempering.

黒糖
Powdered Jaggery

粗い未精製の茶色い砂糖。サトウキビから作られ、固形の状態で入手しやすいですが、調理に使用しやすいよう粉末化されたものもあります。

Also called Gur or molasses, this coarse, brown, unrefined sugar is made from the juice of crushed sugarcane. It is generally available in semi-solid form, which can be powdered for use in cooking.

—豆—
Lentils

トゥール豆
Toor Dal / Red Gram / Pigeon Peas

半分に割れたスプリットタイプの黄色いレンズ豆。南インドの料理で広く使われていて、サンバルやラッサムを作る際、ゆでてクリーム状にして使用されます。

Also known as arhar it is a dal yellow lentil. Widely used in South Indian cooking, it is cooked to a creamy consistency, especially to make sambar and rasam.

ウラド豆
Urad Dal / Black Gram

南インドの料理には欠かせない淡いクリーム色の豆。撹拌するとクリーミーになるのが特徴。皮付きのものと皮を剥いたスプリットタイプがあります。

Also known as white lentils, urad dal is split urad beans with their skin removed. It is essential to South Indian cooking, used both as a Tempering as well a base for dosa and idli.

チャナ豆／ベンガルグラム
Chana Dal / Bengal Gram

側面が丸い面と平らな面のある、皮のないスプリットタイプのレンズ豆。焙煎するとカリカリとした食感になります。テンパリングをはじめ、インド料理に使われる定番の豆です。

Closely related to the chickpea family, chana dal is a split yellow lentil that is rounded on one side and flat on the other. It has a nutty flavor and a crunchy texture, when roasted.

ムング豆（緑・黄）
Moong Dal / Green Gram / Yellow Moong Dal

日本では「緑豆」としても知られているムング豆。緑色のものと黄色いスプリットタイプがあります。消化しやすく、浸水や加熱時間も比較的短いので、調理しやすいのが特徴。

Among the most versatile dals, The green gram dal is split moong beans with its skin. The golden yellow moong dal is made from moong beans that are skinned and split. Moong dal is relatively easy to digest and used in a variety of Indian dishes.

ひよこ豆／チックピー
Chickpeas / Garbanzo Beans

別名「ガルバンゾ」とも呼ばれるひよこ豆。たんぱく質が多く、さまざまな料理に使われます。市販では、乾燥だけでなくローストしたものもあります。

Also known as Gram, they are high in protein. The larger tan variety is called Kabuli chana and smaller kind which comes in green and brown color are called Desi chana or chickpeas.

—米—
Rice

南インドで主食として親しまれている長粒米。多くの種類がありますが、定番の2種類は、日本でも手に入りやすいお米です。

The staple food of South India. There are many varieties of rice in India. I have used long grain rice in this book, as it is easily available in stores in Japan.

プニライス
Pooni Rice

タミル・ナードゥ州とアンドラ・プラデシュ州の品種「プニ」は、長粒米の中でも比較的短く、軽くて芳香性があり、平米風味の米料理に特に適しています。

The medium grain Ponni and Sona Masoori rice from Tamil Nadu and Andhra Pradesh respectively, is light and aromatic and is especially suited to plain and flavored rice dishes.

バスマティライス
Basmati Rice

香りがあり、さまざまな料理に使える長粒米のバスマティライスは、やわらかな食感が特徴。ビリヤニなどの米料理を作るのに適しています。

An aromatic and versatile long grain rice. The cooked grains are soft and fluffy and are especially suited to make flavored rice dishes such as Biryani.

南インド料理の基礎技術
Basic Techniques

── テンパリング ──
Tempering

すべてのインド料理（特に南インド料理）にとって重要な調味料は、「油」です。
『テンパリング』と呼ばれる香味油は、インド料理に欠かせないステップです。

A technique crucial to all Indian cooking, and especially to South Indian cooking is seasoning of the oil.
It is called Tempering in the South and Tarka, Chaunk in the North of India.
This can be the first step or the last step, in making a dish.

テンパリングに使用する豆の準備
Tip for using dal in Tempering

テンパリングに使用するチャナ豆やウラド豆は、あらかじめ10〜15分浸水させて水を切ったものを使用します。
Soak the urad dal and chana dal in water for 10-15 minutes. Drain and use.

基本のテンパリングの作り方
Basic South Indian Tempering

① フライパンに油を入れ加熱し、マスタードシードを加える。
② ウラド豆や鷹の爪、カレーリーフを加え、色が変わり香りが
　 立つまで軽くかき混ぜながら炒める。
③ （ポリヤルやカレーなど）鍋に入った状態もしくはお皿に持った
　 上から油をかけて、お好みでかき混ぜながらいただきます。

① Heat oil in a saucepan, add mustard seeds and
　 allow them to splutter.
② Add urad dal, dried red chilies and curry leaves and stir briefly
　 until the dal changes color.
③ Then, either add the vegetables to it (Poriyal), or pour it over the
　 curry (Kadala Curry).

── 豆の炊き方 ──
Lentils

南インドでは、多くの料理で豆が使用されます。レンズ豆、ムング豆、トゥール豆などは、皮つきの「ホール」と
皮をむき2つに割った「スプリット」があります。特にスプリットは調理時間が短く、
ゆでたり撹拌するとクリーミーになり、さまざまな南インド料理の鍵となる食材です。

Dals are dried split pulses (lentils, beans and peas), high in protein and fibre. Available in many varieties,
dals are a key ingredient in most South Indian dishes.

豆を調理するときのポイント
Tips for Cooking Dal

豆は、あらかじめ浸水することでより早く調理することが
できます。さらに、圧力鍋を使用すれば、調理時間を大幅
に短縮することが可能です。

Dals are easy to cook. A little soaking will help cook them
faster. A pressure cooker is an important cooking tool. It can
reduce the cooking time considerably.

豆の炊き方（ゆで上がり1カップ分）
1/2 cup dal (tool dal, yellow moong dal, green moong dal) - Gives 1 cup creamy dal

〈材料〉豆：1/2 カップ　水：2・1/2 カップ
① 浸水しておいた豆の水を切り、鍋に移す。
② 2・1/2 カップの水を加え、フタをして強火で沸騰させる。
③ フタを少し開き、中火で 20 〜 25 分煮る。
④ ときどき混ぜながら、必要に応じてさらに水を足す。
　 やわらかくクリーミーになったら完成。

① Drain the soaked dal and place in a heavy saucepan.
② Cover with 2-1/2 cups water, and bring to a boil.
③ Keep the lid slightly ajar and simmer for 20-25 minutes.
　 Stir frequently, adding more water if needed.
④ Cook until the dal is soft and has a creamy texture.
　 Set aside without draining.

── 長粒米の炊き方 ──
Steamed rice

カレーやスープなど、南インド伝統料理に欠かせないライス。
長粒米は、炊き方によって水の量が異なるため注意しましょう。

Polished white rice cooks quicker and compliments most of the traditional rice accompaniments - from rasam to sambar better.
Basmati rice and Jasmine rice make a good alternative to long grain rice.

＜ガスコンロの場合＞
長粒米：2カップ　水：5〜7カップ
冷たい水で米を洗い、大きな鍋に入れる。
水5〜7カップを加え、沸騰させて約15〜18分米がやわらかくなる
まで加熱する。余分な水がなくなったら、かきまぜて蒸らして完成。

＜炊飯器の場合＞
長粒米：2カップ　水：4カップ
米を水で洗い、30分浸水させたら水を切り炊飯器に移す。水4カップ
を加えてスイッチを入れます。やわらかくなるまで調理する。

〈Cooking on a Gas stove〉
2 cups long grain rice (200g)
Wash the rice in cold water and place it in a large saucepan. Add
5-7 cups water. Bring to a boil Simmer for about 15-18 minutes, or
until the rice is just soft. Drain the excess water from the rice and set
aside. Fluff the cooked rice with a fork and serve hot.

〈cooking in a Rice cooker〉
2 cups long grain rice　4 cups water
Wash and soak the rice in water for 30 minutes. Drain the water
and transfer to a rice cooker. Add 4 cups water and turn on the
switch. Cook until soft. Fluff up the rice and serve.

使用するキッチン用品
Essential Kitchen Equipment

南インド料理を作る上で必要な調理器具をご紹介します。
This list of equipment will help you prepare South Indian food with ease.

ミキサー	Blender
ブレンダー	Electric mixer
乳鉢・乳棒	Mortar and pestle
大きな鍋	Large wok
サイズの異なるノンスティックパン	Variety of nonstick pans of different sizes
深めのフライパン、ノンスティックパン	Deep frying pan
測定スプーン・カップ	Set of measuring spoons and cup

あると便利な道具
圧力鍋
穴あきおたま
平らなノンスティックパン

Recommended Equipment
Pressure cooker
Idli steamer with the Idli mould
Flat non-stick tava or a flat saucepan.

──レシピの見方──
Measurement

小さじ1	5ml	1 teaspoon
大さじ1	15ml	1 tablespoon
1カップ	200ml(200cc)	1cup

Memo（メモ）
保存の目安やアドバイスなど、調理に
使えるメモを記載しています。

Variation（バリエーション）
材料を変えたり、ひと工夫でさまざまな
バリエーションのレシピを紹介します。

料理をはじめる前に

よい食材を選び、準備する時間を大切にしましょう

新鮮な食材を選ぶことは、料理を美味しく、調理時間を短縮する秘訣です。また、スムーズに調理を進めるために、あらかじめ野菜は切り、使用するスパイスは使いやすくボックスなどに入れて、準備をしておきましょう。調理を円滑かつ迅速に進められます。野菜は前日にカットし、冷蔵庫のジッパー付バッグなどに入れておくと便利です。豆は使用する前日に調理し、冷蔵庫に入れておくと、すぐに使用できます。チャツネは、前日に仕込んでおきましょう。

インド料理＝辛くてスパイシーな味つけではありません

インド料理の大抵の辛みは、チリパウダー（赤唐辛子粉末）を使用している場合が多いですが、必ずしも辛い必要は全くありません。料理にパンチがほしいときに使用してください。レシピの中では、中量の唐辛子を使っています。あなた好みに分量を自由に調整してください。スパイスが好きな人は量を追加してみたり、あまり好きではない人は、そのスパイスを省いてみるなど、工夫をしてみてください。

スパイスや食材の味を覚えていきましょう

材料が不足している場合、代わりのものを入れなければならないというイメージがあるかもしれませんが、インド料理は違います。レシピに記載されている特定のスパイスや材料がないからといって、ストレスは感じないでください。

コンロから鍋をおろす前、そしてお皿に盛り付ける前には、
必ず塩で味をととのえましょう。

塩は、香辛料の風味とテンパリングの香りを引き立たせてくれます。また、せっかくの良い食材も、調味料が足りなければ味気ない料理になってしまいます。もし味気なさを感じた場合、大抵の場合、塩、もしくは少量のレモン汁またはほんの少しのチリパウダーを追加すると、味を調整できるので、試してみてください。

Getting Started
General Tips for South Indian Cooking

Relax and enjoy the cooking process. A little too much or too little will not really change or spoil the taste of the dish so precise measurement of ingredients is not required.

Taking time to prepare the ingredients and having them ready for each recipe goes a long way in reducing the total cooking time. The vegetables can be cut on the previous day and stored in zip lock bags in the refrigerator. Dosa batter can be prepared up to two days ahead of time. Dals for sambar and rasam can be cooked and prepared on the previous day as can Chutneys.

Despite its reputation Indian food does not have to be hot and spicy. Red chili powder and dried red chilies can be added at your discretion. My recipes use a medium amount, but feel free to modify the quantity to suit your taste. If there is a particular spice you enjoy, add a little more of it and reduce the amount or skip the spice that you dont like very much.

Dry powdered coconut or dessicated coconut can be used in place of freshly grated coconut.

Leftover food can be refrigerated for a couple of days, and in fact, it may taste better on the next day.

Before taking a dish off the gas stove, always taste for salt. If the salt is less in a dish, it will taste flat. Salt allows the flavors of the spices and tempering to be highlighted. If you feel something is missing in a dish, a dash of salt, a little lemon juice or a little chili powder usually does the trick.

Curry and Soup

カレー＆スープ

南インドのカレーやシチューは、"マサラ"と呼ばれるスパイスのベースから調理します。たっぷりの野菜やココナッツの旨みと合わせることで、奥行きのある味わいが生まれます。どのレシピでもよいので1つ流れを覚えてしまえば、具を変えたり組み合わせを変えても本格的な味が完成します。最後には、コクと香りを出すテンパリングも欠かさずに。この章では、ごはんとよく合うサンバル、シチュー、スープも一緒にご紹介。インドの食卓では、これらを米料理やライスヌードルと合わせてふるまいます。

Kadala Curry

Chickpea Curry 茶色いひよこ豆のカレー

スパイシーなココナッツグレービーがベースの茶色いひよこ豆を使ったケララ州伝統のカレー。
A traditional curry from Kerala. Brown chickpeas are simmered in spicy roasted coconut gravy.

材料　4人分

黒ひよこ豆（ホール）　150g
玉ねぎ　1個（みじん）
トマト　1個（角切り）
ターメリックパウダー　小さじ1/2
塩　適量
コリアンダーリーフ　適量（みじん）
生姜　適量（細切り）

カダラマサラ

鷹の爪　3〜4本
ウラド豆　小さじ1
コリアンダーシード　小さじ1
クミンシード　小さじ1
にんにく　3片（みじん）
生姜　2枚（スライス）
ココナッツパウダー　1/2カップ

テンパリング

ココナッツオイル　大さじ2
マスタードシード　小さじ1

1 黒ひよこ豆はあらかじめ浸水させ、やわらかくゆでたら豆と煮汁を分けておく。
2 カダラマサラを作る。フライパンにココナッツパウダー以外の材料を入れ、香りが立つまで1〜2分炒る。豆の色が薄茶色に変わったら火を止め、ココナッツパウダーを混ぜて粗熱をとる。
3 ブレンダーに移し、ペースト状に撹拌する。
4 テンパリングをする。別のフライパンにココナッツオイルを入れ、マスタードシードを加えてパチパチはじけたら、玉ねぎを加え2〜3分炒める。さらにトマトを加えてやわらかくなるまで加熱する。
5 3を加え、よく混ぜる。1の豆とターメリックパウダーを加えて混ぜ、塩で味をととのえる。少量の煮汁を加えてお好みのやわらかさになったら沸騰させ、5〜6分煮込んで味をしみ込ませる。
6 器に盛り、コリアンダーリーフと生姜を散らす。
7 温かいごはんやパラタやプリと一緒に食べる。

Serves 4

150g dried brown chickpeas
-or 2-1/2 cups cooked chickpeas
1/2 teaspoon salt
1 medium onion, chopped
1 tomato, chopped
1/2 teaspoon turmeric powder
salt to taste
coriander leaves and ginger julienne to garnish

Kadala Masala

3-4 dried red chilies
1 teaspoon urad dal
1 teaspoon coriander seeds
1 teaspoon cumin seeds
2 small cloves garlic
2 thin slices of ginger
1/2 cup coconut, freshly grated or powdered coconut

Tempering

2 tablespoon coconut oil
1 teaspoon mustard seeds

1 Soak the chickpeas overnight in 3 cups water. Drain and transfer to a saucepan. Add 4-5 cups water, 1/2 teaspoon salt and cook covered for 25-30 minutes over medium heat, until tender. Drain and set aside. Keep the cooking liquid.
2 Prepare Kadala Masala. Heat a saucepan, add dried red chilies, urad dal, coriander seeds, cumin seeds, garlic, and ginger. Dry roast over medium heat for 1-2 minutes, until spices are fragrant and the dal turns golden.
3 Add the grated coconut and stir briefly, until lightly browned. Remove from heat and set place the roasted ingredients in an electric mixer and grind in to a paste, using little water. Set aside.
4 Prepare the Tempering. Heat 2 tablespoon coconut oil in a saucepan, add mustard seeds and allow them to splutter. Add the chopped onion and saute for 2-3 minutes, until soft. Add chopped tomato and cook for another minute.
5 Add the prepared Kadala Masala and the cooked chickpeas. Add turmeric powder, salt to taste, and mix well.
6 Use the reserved cooking liquid to bring to a desired consistency. Bring to a boil and simmer for 5-6 minutes, to allow the spices to blend with the chickpeas.
7 Garnish with coriander leaves and ginger julienne. Serve with Paratha or Poori.

Aviyal

Mixed Vegetables in Coconut and Yogurt Gravy

ココナッツとヨーグルトのカレー

ココナッツオイルとカレーリーフをかけて食べるケララ州のクラシックカレー。
This classic Kerala curry is uniquely flavored with a seasoning of coconut oil and curry leaves.

材料　4人分
お好みの野菜　2カップ（2cm大）
（かぼちゃ、人参、じゃがいも、グリーンピースなど）
ターメリックパウダー　小さじ1/2
塩　適宜
ヨーグルト　1カップ
ココナッツマサラ
ココナッツパウダー　1カップ
青唐辛子　4本
生姜　2枚（スライス）
クミンシード　小さじ1
シーズニング
ココナッツオイル　大さじ1
カレーリーフ　4〜6枚
チリパウダー　小さじ1/4

1 鍋に野菜、ターメリックパウダー、塩を入れ、ひたひたになるくらいの水を加え、6〜7分ほど中火で加熱する。野菜がやわらかくなったら、火からおろす。
2 ココナッツマサラを作る。ブレンダーに材料と少量の水を加えてペースト状に撹拌する。
3 1に2を加える。弱火で3〜4分ほど蒸らす。ヨーグルトを加えてよく混ぜ、塩で味をととのえる。
4 器に盛り、ココナッツオイル、カレーリーフ、チリパウダーをかける。ごはんと合わせて食べる。

メモ：乳製品の使用を避けたい場合は、ヨーグルトの代わりにココナッツミルク1/2カップを使用してください。

Serves 4
2 cups mixed vegetables (pumpkin, carrot, beans, peas),
- cut into 2 cm pieces
1/2 teaspoon turmeric powder
salt to taste
1 cup yogurt
Coconut Masala
1 cup freshly grated coconut or powdered coconut
1 teaspoon cumin seeds
4 green chilies
2 small slices ginger
Seasoning
1 tablespoon coconut oil
4-6 curry leaves, torn
1/4 teaspoon chili powder

1 Place the cut vegetables in a saucepan, add turmeric powder and salt to taste. Add enough water to cover the vegetables and cook over medium heat for 6-7 minutes, until the vegetables are tender. Remove from heat and set aside with its cooking liquid.
2 Prepare the Coconut Masala. Place the grated coconut, cumin seeds, green chilies, and ginger in an electric mixer and grind to a smooth paste, using a little water. Transfer to a bowl and set aside.
3 Add the Coconut Masala paste to the cooked vegetables, 1/2 cup water and mix well. Bring to a boil and simmer for 2-3 minutes. Add the yogurt and cook for another 2-3 minutes, over low heat. Remove from heat.
4 Prepare the Seasoning. Heat the coconut oil in a small saucepan, add curry leaves and let them sizzle. Add chili powder and remove from heat. Pour over the vegetable curry and serve hot with steamed rice.

Memo: Use 1/2 cup coconut milk instead of yogurt, if you wish to avoid the use of dairy products.
The Seasoning step can be omitted, and the coconut oil can be drizzled on the curry.

Kaikari Kurma

Vegetable Korma ベジタブルココナッツカレー

ココナッツをはじめ、フレッシュな野菜とハーブ、ホールスパイスで作る香り豊かなカレー。
Mixed vegetables are cooked in an aromatic gravy made of freshly ground spices, coconut, chilies and fresh coriander.

材料　4人分

玉ねぎ　1/2個（みじん）
トマト　1個（角切り）

A
| カリフラワー　1カップ（小房を分ける）
| 人参　1本（2cm大）
| グリーンピース　1/4カップ
| インゲン豆　8〜10本（1cm大）
| ターメリックパウダー　小さじ1/2
| 塩　適量

ココナッツマサラ
ココナッツパウダー　1/2カップ
生姜　1片
にんにく　1片
青唐辛子　2〜3本
コリアンダーリーフ　1/2カップ（みじん）

ドライマサラ
フェンネルシード　大さじ1
ポピーシード　大さじ1
コリアンダーシード　大さじ1
シナモンスティック　小1本
クローブ　3〜4粒
カルダモン　2粒

テンパリング
ギーまたはお好みの油　大さじ1
ベイリーフ　2枚

1 ココナッツマサラを作る。材料と少量の水をブレンダーに入れ、なめらかなペースト状にする。
2 ドライマサラを作る。フライパンに材料を入れ中火にかけ、1〜2分炒る。香りが立ったらブレンダーに入れ、細かく粉砕する。
3 鍋にAを入れ、ひたひたになるくらいの水を加えてやわらかくなるまで中火で4〜5分煮る。
4 テンパリングをする。フライパンにギーを入れ熱し、ベイリーフ、玉ねぎを加え2〜3分炒める。そこにトマト、2を加え、よく混ぜる。
5 1と水1/2カップを加える。野菜にスープの味がしみ込むまで6〜8分蒸し煮する。コリアンダーリーフをトッピングする。

バリエーション：Aをじゃがいも3個、人参1本に変えて調理するとポテトココナッツカレーになります。

Serves 4

8-10 cauliflower florets
1 carrot, peeled, diced
1/4 cup shelled green peas
8-10 green beans, cut into 1cm pieces
1 onion, finely chopped
1 tomato, chopped
1/2 teaspoon turmeric powder
salt to taste

Coconut Masala
1/2 cup fresh coconut grated or powdered coconut
1 small piace ginger
1 clove garlic
2-3 green chilies
1/4 cup fresh coriander leaves, chopped

Ground Dry Masala
1 tablespoon fennel seeds
1 tablespoon poppy seeds
1 tablespoon coriander seeds
small stick of cinnamom
3-4 cloves
2 cardamom

Tempering
1 tablespoon ghee or oil
2 bay leaves

1 Prepare the vegetables. Place the cauliflower, carrot, beans, green peas in a saucepan and add enough water to cover the vegetables. Add turmeric powder, salt to taste and cook covered for 4-5 minutes over medium heat, until the vegetables are tender. Set aside with the cooking liquid.
2 Prepare the Coconut Masala. Place the coconut, ginger, garlic, green chilies, and coriander leaves in an electric mixer. Blend together to a paste, with 2-3 tablespoon water. Set aside.
3 Prepare the Ground Dry Masala. In a small saucepan, dry roast the fennel seeds, poppy seeds, coriander seeds, cinnamon stick, cloves and cardamom over medium heat for 1-2 minutes, until fragrant. Remove from heat and transfer to an electric mixer. Grind to a fine powder and set aside.
4 Prepare the Tempering. Heat 1 tablespoon oil in a medium saucepan, add bay leaves, chopped onions and saute for 2-3 minutes. Add chopped tomato and stir briefly. Add the Ground Dry Masala and mix well.
5 Add Coconut Masala paste, the cooked vegetables with its remaining cooking liquid and add 1/2 cup water. Mix together, taste for salt and simmer for 6-8 minutes, over medium heat to allow the vegetables to absorb the flavors of the gravy.

Variation：Potato Korma : Use 3 potatoes and 1 carrot, peeled and diced instead of the mixed vegetables and proceed as above.

Poori

Fried Whole Wheat bread プリ（揚げパン）

特別なときにふるまわれる、全粒粉を使用した揚げパン。揚げたときに膨らむのが特徴。

A whole wheat bread that puffs up when deep-fried, Poori is an indulgence reserved for special occasions.

材料　12〜15個分

全粒粉　1・1/2カップ
お好みの油　大さじ1
塩　小さじ1/4
打ち粉　適量
揚げ油　適量

1 ボウルに全粒粉、油、塩を入れ、手でこねる。
2 水約1/3カップを少しずつ加えてこねる。ずっしり重く、指にくっつかなくなったらボウルを湿った布で覆い約10分生地を寝かせる。
3 手に軽く油をつけて2の生地をこね、12〜15等分して丸める。
4 打ち粉をふり、麺棒を使って、生地を1個ずつ直径6〜7cmの円形に伸ばす。生地がくっつかないようクッキングシートの上に並べる。
5 200℃の揚げ油を用意し、4を1〜2個入れ揚げる。沈んだ生地が浮かんできたら、表面をおたまでやさしく突いてボールのように膨らます。
6 生地を裏返して10秒ほどしたら油から上げる。キッチンペーパーの上にすくい油を切る。カレーなどと一緒に食べる。

メモ：低温の揚げ油では生地が膨らまないので注意しましょう。油の温度が下がるため、一度に揚げる量は調整しましょう。こねればこねるほど、美味しく仕上がります。

Makes 12-15

1・1/2 cup whole wheat flour
1 teaspoon oil
1/4 teaspoon salt
flour for dusting
oil for frying

1 Sift the flour in a mixing bowl. Add salt and rub in the oil by hand.
2 Gradually add about 1/3 cup of water, and knead to form a firm but soft dough. Set aside for 10 minutes.
3 Knead the dough again with lightly oiled hands and divide into 12-15 balls. Dab in flour and keep aside.
4 Using a rolling pin, roll out the dough balls into small rounds of 6-7 cm in diameter. Keep the pooris separate, by placing them on a wax paper.
5 Heat the oil for deep frying to 200℃. Slide a poori into the hot oil. It will immediately rise to the surface. Gently press on the sides. The poori will puff up like a ball.
6 Flip it over, using a slotted spoon. After about 10 seconds, remove from the oil and drain on kitchen paper. Repeat the process with the rest of the pooris. Serve hot with Korma or Kadala Curry.

Memo：The poori will only puff up if the oil is hot.
Do not fry multiple pooris at a time. The oil temperature will go down and the pooris will get greasy.
The more you knead the dough, the softer the pooris will be.

Paratha

Flaky Wheat Bread パラタ（平たい全粒粉パン）

平たい全粒粉のパン。具だくさんなカレーとよく合います。

This staple flat bread is a favorite accompaniment to rich curries like Vegetable Korma and Chickpeas Curry.

材料　10～12枚
全粒粉　2カップ
塩　小さじ1/4
ギーまたはお好みの油　適量
打ち粉　適量

Makes 10-12
2 cups whole wheat flour
1/4 teaspoon salt
ghee or oil
flour for dusting

1 ボウルに全粒粉と塩を入れよく混ぜる。水約1/2カップを少しずつ加えて、やわらかい生地になるようよくこねる。ボウルを湿った布で覆い、約10分生地をなじませる。

2 手に軽く油をつけて再び生地をよくこねたら10～12等分に分ける。

3 1個ずつ打ち粉をまぶし、麺棒で均一な厚さになるように直径6～8cmの円形を作り、ハケで表面に油を薄く塗る。

4 再度打ち粉をまぶし、筒状になるように手で生地を丸め、両端を合わせて丸状になるようもとす。

5 再び均一な厚さになるように直径6～8cmに生地を伸ばす。

6 加熱した平たいフライパンに生地を並べ、薄く茶色になるまで両面を焼く。

7 表面にハケで油を塗り、ヘラを使いやさしく押しながらしっかりと焼いていく。裏返し両面がきつね色に焼けたら火からおろす。

8 キッチンペーパーやアルミホイルで包み、保温する。カレーなどと一緒に食べる。

1 In a mixing bowl, combine the flour and salt. Gradually add about 1/2 cup water and knead well to form a soft dough. Cover with a damp cloth and set aside for 10 minutes.

2 Knead the dough again with greased hands and divide into 10-12 walnut size balls. Dab in flour and set aside.

3 Roll out each portion into small rounds of 6-8 cm in diameter. Brush about 1/2 teaspoon of ghee on the surface and sprinkle some flour over it.

4 Roll it like a cigar and round it up to make a ball of dough again. Seal the edges by pressing them together. Repeat with rest of the dough balls and set aside.

5 Roll out each ball again to make a Paratha of 6-8 cm in diameter.

6 Heat a tava, or a flat non-stick pan and cook both sides of the Paratha, until lightly browned.

7 Brush the top with ghee and press on it gently with a spatula. Flip over and cook the other side. When both sides are golden brown, remove from heat. Repeat with the rest of the Parathas.

8 Wrap in a kitchen towel or foil to keep soft and warm. Serve with Korma Curry or Kadala Curry.

Ghee ギー

バターから水分やたんぱく質を取り除き、純粋な油分にしたもの。インドで古くから伝わる予防医学アーユルヴェーダの中でも活用されています。ビタミンA、Eが豊富で、抗酸化効果も高いとされています。主にカレーや米料理、パンやデザートに使用され、この本のレシピの中ではパラタをはじめ、米料理やデザートに登場します。料理に香ばしい風味をプラスします。

A form of clarified butter. In a typical South Indian meal, ghee is always added to hot rice before it is mixed with the rest of the curries. Traditionally, a generous amount of ghee is used in the making of rice dishes, such as Ven Pongal and Bisi Bela Huli Anna. Ghee is also used to prepare desserts such as Rava Kesari and breads such as Paratha.

Vendakkai Igguru

Okra Curry in Coconut milk　ココナッツミルクとオクラのカレー

Potato Saung

Vendakkai Igguru

Okra Curry from Andhra ココナッツミルクとオクラのカレー

ココナッツソースにオクラと玉ねぎ、黒胡椒を加えて作るアンドラ料理です。
Okra and onions in a coconut sauce, spiced with black pepper. A classic Andhra dish.

材料　4人分
お好みの油　大さじ1
オクラ　250g（ヘタをとり2cm大）
玉ねぎ　2個（スライス）
トマト　2個（角切り）
ココナッツミルク　1/2カップ

A
チリパウダー　小さじ1
ターメリックパウダー　小さじ1/4
ガラムマサラ　小さじ1/2
黒胡椒　小さじ1
塩　適量

テンパリング
ココナッツオイル　大さじ2
マスタードシード　小さじ1
にんにく　3〜4片（みじん）
生姜　小さじ1（みじん）
鷹の爪　2本（半分に切る）
カレーリーフ　6〜8枚

Serves 4
250g okra (lady finger)
1 tablespoon oil
2 onions, sliced
1 teaspoon red chili powder
1/4 teaspoon turmeric powder
1/2 teaspoon garam masala
1/2 teaspoon black pepper
2 tomatoes, chopped
salt to taste
1/2 cup coconut milk

Tempering
2 teaspoon coconut oil
1 teaspoon mustard seeds
3-4 cloves garlic, finely chopped
1 teaspoon ginger, finely chopped
2 dried red chilies, halved
6-8 curry leaves

1 フライパンに油をひき、オクラを中火で3〜4分炒め、塩をふり冷ましておく。
2 テンパリングをする。フライパンにココナッツオイルを入れ熱し、マスタードシードを加えパチパチとはじけさせる。残りの材料を加えて中火で1〜2分炒める。
3 玉ねぎを加え、きつね色になるまで3〜4分炒め、Aを加える。
4 トマトとココナッツミルクを加え、煮汁がなじむまで2〜3分中火にかける。
5 1を加え、よく混ぜる。ごはんやパラタと一緒に食べる。

1 Top the okra and cut into 2 cm pieces. Heat 1 tablespoon oil in a saucepan and saute the okra briefly. Add salt to taste and cook for 3-4 minutes, over medium heat
2 Prepare the Tempering. Heat 2 teaspoon coconut oil in a flat saucepan, add mustard seeds and let them splutter. Add chopped garlic, ginger, dried red chilies, curry leaves and saute for 1-2 minutes, over medium heat.
3 Add the sliced onion and saute for 3-4 minutes until they turn light brown. Add red chili powder, turmeric powder, garam masala, and ground black pepper
4 Add the chopped tomatoes and stir. Allow its liquid to mix with the spices.
5 Finally, add the coconut milk, sauteed okra and simmer for 2-3 minutes over medium heat, until the sauce is absorbed by the okra. Serve hot with steamed rice or Paratha.

Urulaikizhangu Saung

Spicy Potatoes with Tamarind and Jaggery じゃがいものドライカレー

ココナッツオイルの香りが特徴的なカレー。日本の肉じゃがのような甘い味わい。
A classic Konkan curry which gets its distinct flavor from coconut oil used in the tempering.

材料　4人分

じゃがいも　大4個（皮をむき一口大）
玉ねぎ　3個（みじん）
塩　適量
コリアンダーリーフ（みじん）

テンパリング

ココナッツオイル　大さじ2
マスタードシード　小さじ1
カレーリーフ　6〜8枚

A
| タマリンドペースト　大さじ2
| チリパウダー　小さじ1
| 黒糖　大さじ1・1/2
| コリアンダーパウダー　小さじ1・1/2

1　じゃがいもをやわらかくなるまでゆで、ザルにあける。
2　テンパリングをする。フライパンにココナッツオイルを入れ熱し、マスタードシードとカレーリーフを加える。
3　パチパチはじけたら玉ねぎを加え、中火できつね色になるまで3〜4分炒める。
4　1を加え、玉ねぎとなじむまで2〜3分炒める。
5　Aを加え、よく混ぜてからフタをして3〜4分加熱する。
6　仕上げにコリアンダーリーフをトッピングして完成。ライスヌードルやプリ、ごはんなどと合わせて食べる。

Serves 4

4 large potatoes, boiled
3 onions, finely chopped
salt to taste
1 tablespoon tamarind pulp
1 teaspoon chili powder
1 · 1/2 tablespoon jaggery
1 · 1/2 teaspoon coriander powder
coriander leaves, chopped to garnish

Tempering

2 tablespoon coconut oil
1 teaspoon mustard seeds
6-8 curry leaves

1　Place the potatoes in a saucepan, add 4-5 cups water and bring to a boil. Cook for 8-10 minutes on medium heat, until tender. Drain and set aside to cool. Peel the skin and mash the potatoes. Set aside.
2　Prepare the Tempering. Heat 2 tablespoon coconut oil in a flat saucepan. Add mustard seeds, curry leaves and allow the seeds to splutter.
3　Add the chopped onions and saute for 3-4 minutes, on medium heat, until lightly browned.
4　Add the potatoes, salt to taste and saute for another 2-3 minutes, until the potatoes are well coated with the onions.
5　Add the tamarind pulp, chili powder, jaggery and coriander powder. Mix well and cook covered for 3-4 minutes, until the spices have blended with the potatoes.
6　Garnish with coriander leaves and serve hot with Poori or steamed rice.

Garam Masala　ガラムマサラ

材料　1/2カップ

A
| コリアンダーシード　大さじ3
| クミンシード　大さじ2
| カルダモン　大さじ2
| 黒胡椒　大さじ2
| シナモンスティック　1本
| クローブ　大さじ1杯
| フェヌグリーク種　小さじ1
ナツメグパウダー　小さじ1
生姜パウダー　小さじ1
ターメリックパウダー　小さじ1

平らなフライパンを熱し、Aを入れて中火で2〜3分炒る。軽く茶色になったら火からおろし、ブレンダーで撹拌する。ボウルに移し、残りのスパイスを混ぜる。密閉して保存をする。

Makes 1/2 cup

3 tablespoon coriander seeds	1 tablespoon whole cloves
2 tablespoon cumin seeds	1 teaspoon fenugreek seeds
2 tablespoon cardamom seeds	1 teaspoon nutmeg powder
2 tablespoon black peppercorn	1 teaspoon dried ginger powder
1 small stick cinnamon	1 teaspoon turmeric powder

Heat a flat saucepan, place the coriander seeds, cumin seeds, cardamom seeds, black peppercorn, cinnamon stick, cloves, fenugreek seeds and dry roast over medium heat for 2-3 minutes, until fragrant and lightly browned. Remove from heat and transfer to an electric mixer. Grind to a smooth powder. Transfer to a bowl. Add the nutmeg powder, ginger powder and turmeric powder. Mix well and store in an airtight container.

Ennai Kathirikkai

Stuffed Eggplant なすのドライカレー

タミル・ナドゥー州で愛されるドライカレー。ピーナッツとゴマのクリスピー生地が特徴。
A favorite of Tamil Nadu. Small eggplant stuffed with roasted spices, ground peanuts and sesame seeds.

材料　4人分
ココナッツパウダー　カップ1/2
タマリンドペースト　小さじ1/2
塩　適量
なす　小400g
コリアンダーリーフ　適量
ココナッツパウダー　適量

マサラ（詰め物）
A
　お好みの油　大さじ1
　コリアンダーシード　大さじ1
　ピーナッツ　大さじ2
　ゴマ　大さじ2
　鷹の爪　2〜3本
　アサファティーダパウダー　小さじ1/4

テンパリング
お好みの油　大さじ2
マスタードシード　小さじ1
クミンシード　小さじ1
カレーリーフ　4〜6枚

Serves 4
400g small eggplant

Masala for Stuffing
1 tablespoon oil
1 tablespoon coriander seeds
2 tablespoon peanuts
2 tablespoon sesame seeds
2-3 dried red chilies
1/4 teaspoon asafoetida powder
1/2 cup fresh coconut, grated or powdered coconut
1/4 teaspoon tamarind paste
salt to taste
coriander leaves for garnish

Tempering
2 tablespoon oil
1 teaspoon mustard seeds
1 teaspoon cumin seeds
4-6 curry leaves

1 マサラを作る。鍋にAを入れ、中火で数分炒める。

2 1をブレンダーに移し、ココナッツパウダー、タマリンドペースト、塩、少量の水を加え、滑らかなペースト状になるまで撹拌する。

3 なすに縦に包丁を入れ、完全に切り取らないようスリットを作る。スリットに2を均一な厚さに挟み込む。残ったマサラは分けておく。

4 テンパリングをする。大きめの平たいフライパンに油を入れ熱し、材料を加えたらパチパチとはじけるまでかき混ぜながら加熱する。

5 3のなすを並べ、塩で味をつける。少量の水を振りかけ、かき混ぜながら8〜10分加熱する。残りのマサラをふりかけ、さらに2〜3分加熱する。

6 コリアンダーリーフとココナッツパウダーをトッピングする。ごはんやパラタと食べる。

1 Prepare the Masala for Stuffing. Heat 1 tablespoon oil in a saucepan, place coriander seeds, peanuts, sesame seeds, dried red chilies, asafoetida powder and saute over medium heat for a couple of minutes.

2 Add the coconut and stir briefly. Remove from heat and transfer to an electric mixer. Add the tamarind, salt to taste and grind to a smooth paste, using a little water. Set aside.

3 Make two vertical slits on the eggplants, without cutting them through entirely. Fill the slits with the stuffing and keep aside. Keep the left over stuffing aside.

4 Prepare the Tempering: Heat 2 tablespoon oil in a saucepan, on medium heat. Add the mustard seeds, cumin seeds, and curry leaves. Let the mustard seeds splutter.

5 Add the stuffed eggplant and add salt to taste. Sprinkle a little water over the eggplant and cook covered for 8-10 minutes, stirring occasionally until the eggplant is well cooked. Sprinkle the leftover masala over the eggplant and cook further 2-3 minutes. Remove from heat.

6 Garnish with coriander leaves and sprinkle with grated coconut. Serve hot with plain rice or Paratha.

Erissery

Yellow Pumpkin Curry　かぼちゃカレー

ローストしたココナッツとスパイスを使用して作るケララ州の古典的なシチュー。
This traditional stew from Kerala is a fragrant blend of roasted coconut and spices.

材料　4人分
かぼちゃ　400g（皮をむき角切り）
ターメリックパウダー　小さじ1/2
塩　少々
ココナッツパウダー　大さじ1

ココナッツマサラ
クミンシード　小さじ1
鷹の爪　1本
ココナッツパウダー　1カップ

テンパリング
お好みの油　大さじ1
マスタードシード　小さじ1
鷹の爪　1本
カレーリーフ　4〜6枚

1 ココナッツマサラを作る。ブレンダーに材料と少量の水を入れ、ペースト状に撹拌する。
2 鍋にかぼちゃ、ターメリックパウダー、塩を入れ、ひたひたになるまで水を入れ、中火で8〜10分加熱する。
3 1と2を合わせる。水を加え、お好みのやわらかさにする。
4 テンパリングをする。フライパンに油を入れ熱し、材料を加える。パチパチとはじけて豆の色が変わるまでかき混ぜながら炒める。
5 3にココナッツパウダーを加え、テンパリングした油をかける。ごはんを添えて食べる。

バリエーション：かぼちゃの代わりにじゃがいもと人参を使って作ることもできます。

Serves 4
400g pumpkin, peeled and cubed
1 tablespoon powdered coconut
1/2 teaspoon turmeric powder
salt to taste

Coconut Masala
1 teaspoon cumin seeds
1 dried red chili
1 cup fresh coconut grated or powdered coconut

Tempering
1 tablespoon oil
1 teaspoon mustard seeds
1 dried red chili
4-6 curry leaves
I table spoon dried shredded coconut

1 Prepare the Coconut Masala. Place the cumin seeds, dried red chili and 1 cup coconut in an electric mixer, and grind to a smooth paste using 2-3 tablespoon of water. Transfer to a bowl.
2 Place the pumpkin in a saucepan and add enough water to cover it completely. Add salt to taste and turmeric powder. Cover and cook for 8-10 minutes, over medium heat, until the pumpkin is tender.
3 Add the Coconut Masala to the cooked pumpkin and mix gently. Add a little water, if the curry seems too dry.
4 Prepare the Tempering. Heat 1 tablespoon oil in a saucepan, add mustard seeds and let them splutter. Add dried red chili, curry leaves, shreded coconut and stir briefly until the coconut is slightly browned.
5 Pour the Tempering over the pumpkin curry and mix well. Serve hot with steamed rice.

Variation : Erissery can also be made using potato and carrot, instead of pumpkin.

Masala Paste　マサラペースト

南インド料理では、スパイスやマサラ（香辛料）をココナッツなどと合わせて調理する"マサラペースト"は重要なプロセスの一つです。乾いた香辛料を焙煎するこの調理法は、スパイスの風味を増すとともに、その苦味をやわらげてくれる役割があります。南インドのキッチンでは、焙煎したスパイスを石の乳棒で挽き、少量の水を使用して濃厚なペーストを作ります。砥石がない場合でも、ブレンダーやミルがあれば、同様に調理することが可能です。

A key process in South Indian cooking is preparing the Masala Paste with roasted spices and coconut. Dry roasting of spices enhances its flavors. In a South Indian kitchen, the spices are freshly roasted and ground on a flat grinding stone with a large stone pestle, to produce a thick paste using minimal water. An electric mixer or blender will do the job just as well, in the absence of the grinding stone.

Pachakari Stew

Vegetable Stew　ベジタブルシチュー

野菜たっぷりのケララ州の古典的なシチュー。ココナッツミルクとホールスパイスが奥行きのある味わいです。
A classic Kerala stew of mixed vegetables steeped in coconut milk and flavored with whole spices.

材料　4人分

じゃがいも　2個（3cm大）
カリフラワー　100g（小房を分ける）
人参　1本（3cm大）
インゲン豆　50g（3cm大）
ココナッツミルク　2カップ
塩　適量

シチューマサラ

フェンネルシード　小さじ1
クミンシード　小さじ1
コリアンダーシード　小さじ2
鷹の爪　2本
黒胡椒　10〜12粒
ひよこ豆（ロースト）　大さじ1

テンパリング

ココナッツオイル　大さじ1
ベイリーフ　1枚
カルダモン　2粒
シナモンスティック　小1本
クローブ　4〜5粒

A 「玉ねぎ　1個（スライス）
　 青唐辛子　2本（スライス）
　 生姜　大さじ1（千切り）

1 野菜を準備する。鍋にたっぷりのお湯を沸かし、じゃがいもと塩を加えて3〜4分ゆでる。カリフラワー、人参、インゲン豆を加え、さらに3〜4分加熱し湯切りしておく。
2 シチューマサラを作る。フライパンに材料を入れ、香りが出るまで中火で2〜3分煎る。ブレンダーに移し、細かく粉砕する。
3 テンパリングをする。フライパンにココナッツオイルを入れ加熱し、材料を加え、香りが立つまで混ぜながら炒める。
4 Aを加え、玉ねぎが半透明になるまで中火で3〜4分間炒める。
5 2を加え、1〜2分加熱したらココナッツミルクと塩を加えてかき混ぜる。
6 1を加え、中火で2〜3分煮て器に盛る。ごはんや、プリやパラタを添えて食べる。

メモ：シチューマサラを入れなくてもシンプルでおいしいシチューができます。
ローストひよこ豆の粉を入れると、ボリュームのあるシチューになります。

Serves 4

2 potatoes, peeled, cut into 3 cm pieces
1 carrot, peeled, cut into 3 cm pieces
1 cup cauliflower florets
8-10 green beans, cut into 3 cm pieces
1 onion, sliced thin
1 green chili, slit
1 tablespoon ginger, cut into julienne
2 cup coconut milk
salt to taste

Stew Masala

1 teaspoon fennel seeds
1 teaspoon cumin seeds
2 teaspoon coriander seeds
2 dried red chilies
10-12 black peppercorn
1 tablespoon roasted gram

Tempering

1 tablespoon coconut oil
1 bay leaf
2 cardamom
small stick of cinnamon
4-5 cloves

1 Prepare the vegetables. In a saucepan, bring 3-4 cups of water to a boil with a little salt. Add the potatoes and cook for 3-4 minutes. When they are half cooked, add the carrots, beans and cook further 3-4 minutes, until tender. Strain the vegetables and set aside.
2 Prepare the Stew Masala. Heat a flat saucepan and dry roast fennel seeds, cumin seeds, coriander seeds, dried red chilies, peppercorns, and roasted gram for 2-3 minutes, over medium heat until fragrant. Transfer to an electric mixer, grind to a smooth powder and set aside.
3 Prepare the Tempering. Heat 1 tablespoon coconut oil in a saucepan. Add bay leaf, cardamom, cinnamon stick, cloves and stir briefly.
4 Add the sliced onions, green chili, ginger julienne and saute for 3-4 minutes over medium heat, until the onions turn translucent.
5 Add the ground Stew Masala and saute for 1-2 minutes. Add cooked vegetables and stir to mix. Add coconut milk and salt to taste. Mix well.
6 The vegetables should be steeped in the coconut milk. Simmer for 3-4 minutes over medium heat. Transfer to a serving dish. Serve with steamed rice, Poori or Paratha.

Memo : For a simpler yet tasty Stew. Skip the Stew Masala and proceed as above.
The powdered roasted gram adds volume to the stew.

Vengaya Sambar

Pearl Onion Sambar ベビーオニオンサンバル

ベビーオニオンを使った定番の濃厚なスープ。ティフィンと一緒に食卓に並びます。

Best served with steamed rice, Vengaya sambar compliments most breakfast dishes such as Dosa and Ven Pongal.

材料　4人分

トゥール豆　1/2カップ

お好みの油　大さじ1

ベビーオニオン　18〜20個（皮をむく）

タマリンドペースト　小さじ1/2

トマトピューレ　1カップ

黒糖　小さじ1

ターメリックパウダー　小さじ1/2

塩　適量

コリアンダーリーフ　適量

ココナッツマサラ

お好みの油　大さじ1

A
チャナ豆　大さじ1
鷹の爪　2本
黒胡椒　8〜10粒
フェヌグリーグシード　小さじ1/2

B
コリアンダーシード　大さじ2
ココナッツパウダー　大さじ3
アサファティーダパウダー　1つまみ

テンパリング

お好みの油　小さじ1

マスタードシード　小さじ1

鷹の爪　1本

カレーリーフ　4〜6枚

1 トゥール豆をよく洗い、2カップの水と鍋に入れ、クリーム状になるまで15〜20分煮る。

2 ココナッツマサラを準備する。フライパンに油を入れ加熱し、Aを加えたら豆に色がつくまで中火で炒める。Bを加え、香りが立つまでさらに1分炒める。火から下ろして冷ましておく。

3 2をブレンダーに移し、少量の水を加えペースト状に撹拌する。

4 鍋に油を入れ加熱し、ベビーオニオンを加え、2〜3分炒める。タマリンドペースト、トマトピューレ、黒糖、ターメリックパウダー、塩を加える。

5 ココナッツマサラ、1を煮汁ごと加えてよく混ぜる。水1カップを加えて塩で味をととのえ、中火で4〜5分加熱して沸騰させる。

6 テンパリングをする。フライパンに油を入れ加熱し、材料を加えてマスタードシードがパチパチはじけるまでかき混ぜながら炒める。5の上に注いでよく混ぜる。器に盛り、コリアンダーリーフを飾って完成。

メモ：炒めた玉ねぎ4〜5個をココナッツマサラの材料に加えると、より濃厚なサンバルに仕上がります。

Serves 4

1/2 cup toor dal

1 tablespoon oil

18-20 baby onion, peeled

1/2 teaspoon tamarind paste

1 cup tomato puree

1 teaspoon jaggery

1/2 teaspoon turmeric powder

salt to taste

coriander leaves to garnish

Coconut Masala

1 tablespoon oil

1 tablespoon chana dal

1/2 teaspoon fenugreek seeds

8-10 black peppercorns

2 dried red chilies

2 tablespoon coriander seeds

3 tablespoon grated coconut, fresh or powdered coconut

pinch of asafoetida powder

Tempering

1 teaspoon oil

1 teaspoon mustard seeds

1 dried red chili

4-6 curry leaves

1 Wash and place the toor dal in a saucepan. Add 2 cups water and cook for 15-20 minutes, until creamy in texture. Mix and set aside with its cooking liquid.

2 Prepare the Coconut Masala. Heat 1 tablespoon oil in a saucepan, add chana dal, fenugreek seeds, peppercorns anddried red chilies. Stir briefly over medium heat until the dal turns golden. Add coriander seeds, asafatida powder, grated coconut and stir for a minute until fragrant. Remove from heat and cool.

3 Place the above roasted ingredients in an electric mixer and blend to a smooth paste, using a little water. Set aside.

4 To Proceed. Heat 1 tablespoon oil in a saucepan. Add shallots and saute for 2-3 minutes. Add tamarind paste, tomato puree, jaggery, turmeric powder and salt to taste. Stir to mix.

5 Add the Coconut Masala paste, cooked toor dal along with its cooking liquid and mix well. Add 1 cup of water and salt to taste. Bring to a boil and simmer for 4-5 minutes, over medium heat.

6 Prepare the Tempering. Heat 1 teaspoon oil in a skillet, add mustard seeds, dried red chilies and curry leaves. Allow the mustard seeds to splutter. Pour the tempering over the sambar and mix well. Serve hot.

Memo : Add 4-5 shallots to the Coconut Masala. Saute the shallots with the rest of the spices and proceed as above. This will give a thicker and fuller consistency to the sambar.

Gobi Sambar

Cauliflower Sambar カリフラワーサンバル

ローストスパイスを使用した伝統的なサンバルスープ。
Freshly roasted spices add a rich flavor to this delightful variation of the traditional sambar.

材料　4人分

トゥール豆　1/2カップ
カリフラワー　200g（小房を分ける）
トマト　2個（角切り）
ターメリックパウダー　小さじ1/2
サンバルパウダー　小さじ2
塩　適量
ピーマン　1個（スライス）

マサラペースト

お好みの油　小さじ1
ココナッツパウダー　大さじ2

A
ウラド豆　小さじ1
鷹の爪　3〜4本
玉ねぎ　1/2個（みじん）
コリアンダーシード　小さじ1
フェヌグリークシード　小さじ1/2
アサファティーダパウダー　1つまみ

テンパリング

お好みの油　小さじ2
マスタードシード　小さじ1
鷹の爪　1本（半分に切る）
カレーリーフ　4〜6枚

1 トゥール豆をよく洗い、水2カップと鍋に入れ、クリーム状になるまで15〜20分煮る。

2 マサラペーストを作る。フライパンに油を入れ加熱し、Aを加えて2〜3分かき混ぜながら炒める。香りが立ったらココナッツパウダーを加えてさっとかき混ぜる。火から下ろし、粗熱をとる。

3 2をブレンダーに移し、少量の水を加えペースト状に撹拌する。

4 鍋にカリフラワーを入れ、ひたひたになるまで水を加えたらトマト、ターメリックパウダー、サンバルパウダー、塩を入れ、野菜がやわらかくなるまで、5〜7分加熱する。

5 ピーマン、マサラペースト、煮たトゥール豆を煮汁ごと加えてよく混ぜる。お好みで水を加え、中火で4〜5分加熱しする。

6 テンパリングをする。フライパンに油を入れ加熱し、材料を加える。パチパチはじけたら5に入れて混ぜる。ごはんと合わせて食べる。

Serves 4

1/2 cup toor dal
200g cauliflower, cut into florets
1/2 teaspoon tamarind paste
1/2 teaspoon jaggery
2 tomatoes, chopped
1 green pepper, deseeded and sliced
1/2 teaspoon turmeric powder
salt to taste
2 teaspoon sambar powder

Masala Paste

1 teaspoon oil
1 teaspoon urad dal
3-4 dried red chilies
1/2 onion, chopped
1teaspoon coriander seeds
1/2 teaspoon fenugreek seeds
pinch of asafatida powder
2 table spoon fresh grated coconut or powdered coconut

Tempering

2 teaspoon oil
1 teaspoon mustard seeds
1 dried red chili, halved
4-6 curry leaves

1 Wash and place the toor dal in a saucepan. Add 2 cups water and cook for 15-20 minutes, over medium heat until creamy in texture. Mix and set aside with its cooking liquid.

2 Prepare the Masala Paste. Heat the oil in a saucepan, and add urad dal, dried red chilies, chopped onion, coriander seeds, fenugreek seeds and asafoetida powder. Saute for 2-3 minutes, until the spices are fragrant. Add grated coconut and stir briefly. Remove from heat and cool.

3 Place the roasted masala mixture in an electric blender and grind to a smooth paste, adding a little water. Transfer to a bowl and set aside.

4 Place the cauliflower florets in a heavy saucepan, and add enough water to cover. Add tomatoes, turmeric powder, salt to taste and cook covered for 5-7 minutes, until the vegetables are tender.

5 Add tamarind paste, jaggery, green peppers, sambar powder and the prepared Masala. Add the cooked toor dal with the cooking liquid. Mix well and add little water to bring to a desired consistency. Simmer for 3-4 minutes over medium heat.

6 Prepare the Tempering. Heat 2 teaspoon oil in a small saucepan, add mustard seeds, dried red chili and few curry leaves. When the mustard seeds splutter, pour the Tempering over to the sambar and mix. Serve hot with steamed rice.

Kaykari Sambar

Okra, Eggplant and Pumpkin Sambar

ミックスベジタブルサンバル

濃厚な野菜スープは、どのスナックやティフィンとも相性抜群。
A fiery and thick soup of lentil and vegetables, served piping hot with steamed rice.

材料　4人分

トゥール豆　1/2カップ
お好みの油　適量
オクラ　6〜8本（2センチ幅）
玉ねぎ　中1個（みじん）
なす　小1本（一口大）
人参　1/2本（皮をむき一口大）
かぼちゃ　1カップ（皮をむき一口大）
青唐辛子　1本（スライス）
ターメリックパウダー　小さじ1/2
塩　適量
サンバルパウダー　小さじ2
タマリンドペースト　小さじ1/2
トマトビューレ　1カップ
コリアンダーシード（ロースト）　適量
コリアンダーリーフ　適量

テンパリング

お好みの油　大さじ1
マスタードシード　小さじ1
フェヌグリークシード　小さじ1/2
クミンシード　小さじ1/2
鷹の爪　2本（半分に切る）
アサファティーダパウダー　1つまみ
カレーリーフ　4〜6枚

1 トゥール豆をよく洗い、2カップの水と鍋に入れ、クリーム状になるまで15〜20分煮て混ぜておく。
2 フライパンに油を入れ加熱し、オクラを炒める。3〜4分経ったら塩を混ぜる。
3 テンパリングをする。フライパンに油を入れ加熱し、材料を加えてパチパチはじけるまでかき混ぜながら炒める。
4 玉ねぎ、なす、人参、かぼちゃを加え2〜3分炒める。水1・1/2カップ、青唐辛子、ターメリックパウダー、塩を入れ、野菜がやわらかくなるまでフタをして6〜8分ほど煮る。
5 サンバルパウダー、タマリンドペースト、トマトビューレを加えて煮詰める。1を煮汁ごと加えてよく混ぜ、お好みで水を加え、中火でさらに4〜5分加熱する。
6 オクラ、コリアンダーシードを加えて混ぜる。コリアンダーリーフを飾りイドリー、ワダ、ドーサやごはんと合わせて食べる。

バリエーション：ココナッツパウダー大さじ2を足すと、ココナッツのフレーバーが楽しめます。

Serves 4

1/2 cup toor dal
1/2 teaspoon tamarind paste
1 cup tomato puree
1 tablespoon oil
6-8 okra, cut into 2 cm pieces
1 medium onion, peeled and chopped
1 small eggplant, cut into small pieces
1/2 carrot, peeled and cut into 2 cm pieces
1 cup pumpkin, peeled, cut into 2cm pieces
1 green chili, slit
1/2 teaspoon turmeric powder
2 teaspoon sambar powder
salt to taste
1 teaspoon coriander seeds, roasted and ground
1 tablespoon coriander leaves

Tempering

1 tablespoon oil
1 teaspoon mustard seeds
1/2 teaspoon fenugreek seeds
1/2 teaspoon cumin seeds
2 dried red chilies, halved
pinch of asafoetida powder
few curry leaves

1 Wash and place the toor dal in 2 cups of water. Cook for 20-25 minutes, until creamy in texture. Mix and set aside with its cooking liquid.
2 Heat 1 tablesoon oil in a saucepan, and saute the okra for 3-4 minutes. Add a dash of salt and mix. Set aside.
3 Prepare the Tempering: Heat 1 tablespoon oil in a saucepan. Add mustard seeds, fenugreek seeds, cumin seeds, dried red chilies, asafoetida powder, curry leaves and stir briefly. Allow the mustard seeds to splutter.
4 Add the chopped onion, eggplant, carrot, pumpkin and saute for 3-4 minutes. Add 1·1/2 cups water, slit green chili, turmeric powder and salt to taste. Cook covered for 6-8 minutes, until the vegetables are tender.
5 Add the sambar powder, tamarind pulp, tomato puree and bring to a boil. Add the cooked dal with its cooking liquid. Mix well, adding a little water to bring to desired consistency. Simmer over medium heat for 4-5 minutes,
6 Add the sauteed okra and ground coriander seeds. Mix well.
7 Garnish with coriander leaves and serve hot with Idli, Vada, Dosa or steamed rice.

Variation: For Coconut Sambar, grind the Sambar Masala with 2 tablespoon of grated coconut and add to above.

Sambar Powder サンバルパウダー

材料　100g

コリアンダーシード　3/4カップ
鷹の爪　10 ～ 12本
クミンシード　大さじ2
フェヌグリークシード　大さじ3/4
黒胡椒　大さじ3/4
チャナ豆　大さじ2
ウラド豆　大さじ1
トゥール豆　大さじ1
カレーリーフ　8 ～ 10枚
アサファティーダパウダー　小さじ1杯
ターメリックパウダー　小さじ2

フライパンを中火で加熱し、ターメリックパウダー以外の材料をすべて加え、2 ～ 3分フライパンをゆすりながら炒る。香りが立ち色が変わったら火からおろし粗熱をとる。ブレンダーに移して撹拌する。ターメリックパウダーを混ぜ、密閉容器に保管する。

Makes 100g

3/4 cup coriander seeds
10-12 dried red chilies
2 tablespoon cumin seeds
3/4 tablespoon fenugreek seeds
3/4 tablespoon black peppercorns
2 table spoon chana dal
1 table spoon urad dal
1 table spoon toor dal
8-10 curry leaves-opt
1 teaspoon asafoetida powder
2 teaspoon turmeric powder

Heat a broad saucepan, and dry roast all the above ingredients, except the turmeric powder over medium heat. Keep stirring for 2-3 minutes until fragrant and slightly colored. Remove from heat and cool. Place in an electric mixer and grind to a fine powder. Mix in the turmeric powder and store the masala in an air- tight container. Use as needed.

Thakkali Rasam

Tomato Rasam　ラッサム（トマトスープ）

軽くて消化のしやすい、南インドの最も家庭的なスープ。ごはんと一緒にふるまわれます。

Hot and spicy, yet light and easy to digest. A staple in the South Indian home, Rasam is a must-have item with steamed rice.

材料　4人分

タマリンドペースト　小さじ1/2
トゥール豆　1/4カップ
塩　適量
コリアンダーリーフ　適量

A
| トマト　300g（角切り）
| 生姜　1片（すりおろし）
| ラッサムパウダー　小さじ2
| ターメリックパウダー　小さじ1/4

テンパリング

ギーまたはお好みの油　大さじ1
マスタードシード　小さじ1/2
クミンシード　小さじ1/2
黒胡椒　6〜8粒
鷹の爪　1本（半分に切る）
アサファティーダパウダー　1つまみ
カレーリーフ　4〜6枚

1 タマリンドペーストは、水2カップに混ぜておく。トゥール豆は、水2カップと鍋に入れてクリーム状になるまで15〜20分煮る。
2 テンパリングをする。フライパンにギーを入れ、材料を加える。パチパチとはじけるまでかき混ぜながら加熱する。
3 テンパリングをしたフライパンに1、A、塩、水1カップを加えて中火で15〜20分煮る。
4 必要に応じて水を加えてお好みの濃度にして沸騰させる。コリアンダーリーフを飾り、ごはんと一緒に食べる。

メモ：缶詰のトマトでも作ることができます。その場合はつぶしてから使いましょう。

Serves 4

1/2 teaspoon tamarind paste
1/4 cup toor dal
300g fresh tomato, chopped
1 teaspoon ginger, grated
2 teaspoon rasam powder
1/4 teaspoon turmeric powder
salt to taste
coriander leaves to garnish

Tempering

1 tablespoon ghee or oil
1/2 teaspoon mustard seeds
1/2 teaspoon cumin seeds
6-8 black peppercorns, coarsely ground
1 dried red chili, halved
pinch of asafoetida powder
4-6 curry leaves

1 Blend the tamarind paste in 2 cups of water and set aside. Cook toor dal in 2 cups water for 15-20 minutes, over medium heat until creamy.
2 Prepare the Tempering. Heat 1 tablespoon ghee in a saucepan. Add mustard seeds, cumin seeds, ground peppercorn, dried red chili, asafoetida powder and curry leaves. Stir briefly until the mustard seeds splutter.
3 Add the tamarind water and the tomatoes. Add 1 cup water, grated ginger, rasam powder, turmeric powder and salt to taste. Bring to a boil and simmer for 5-7 minutes, over medium heat.
4 Add the cooked dal with its cooking liquid and bring to a boil. Mix well and taste for salt. Simmer for 4-5 minutes. Garnish with coriander leaves.

Memo：If using canned tomatoes, coarsely puree the tomatoes and proceed as per recipe above.

Rasam Powder　ラッサムパウダー

材料 100g

お好みの油　小さじ1
黒胡椒　小さじ1・1/2
クミンシード　小さじ1
トゥール豆　大さじ3
チャナ豆　大さじ3
鷹の爪　9〜10本
アサファティーダパウダー　小さじ1/4

フライパンに油を入れ加熱し、材料を入れ、豆の色が変わるまで炒める。粗熱をとりブレンダーに入れなめらかに撹拌する。密閉容器に入れて保存する。

Makes 100g

1 teaspoon oil
1·1/2 teaspoon whole peppercorns
1 teaspoon cumin seeds
3 tablespoon toor dal
3 tablespoon chana dal
9-10 dried red chili
1/4 teaspoon asafoetida powder

Heat 1 teaspoon oil in a skillet. Add all the above ingredients and saute briefly until the dal changes color. Cool and transfer to an electric mixer. Blend to a fine powder and store in an air tight container. Use as needed.

Mysore Rasam

Coconut and Lentil Rasam　マイソルラッサム（ココナッツと豆のスープ）

たっぷりのスパイスとまろやかなココナッツミルクがやさしい味わい。
Thicker than its watery counterparts and full of flavor from freshly grounded spices. Coconut milk lends a gentle touch.

材料　4人分
タマリンドペースト　小さじ1
トゥール豆　1/2カップ
トマト　300g（角切り）
ラッサムパウダー　小さじ3〜4
黒糖　大さじ1
ターメリックパウダー　小さじ1/2
塩　適量
ココナッツミルク　1カップ
コリアンダーリーフ　適量

テンパリング
ギーまたはお好みの油　大さじ1
マスタードシード　小さじ1
クミンシード　小さじ1
鷹の爪　1本
アサファティーダパウダー　1つまみ
カレーリーフ　4〜6枚

1 タマリンドペーストは、水2カップに混ぜておく。
2 トゥール豆を洗い、水2〜3カップの水で20〜30分やわらかくなるまで煮て、よく混ぜる。
3 テンパリングをする。フライパンにギーを入れ加熱し、材料を加える。パチパチはじけるまで炒める。
4 1、トマト、ラッサムパウダー、黒糖、ターメリックパウダー、塩を加えてよく混ぜ、5〜7分煮込む。
5 2を入れて混ぜ、4〜5分中火で煮込む。
6 ココナッツミルク、コリアンダーリーフを加えて、沸騰させる。ごはんやパパドと一緒に食べる。

Serves 4
1 teaspoon tamarind paste
1/2 cup toor dal
3 tomatoes, chopped
3-4 teaspoon Mysore Rasam powder
1 tablespoon jaggery
1/2 teaspoon turmeric powder
salt to taste
1 cup coconut milk
coriander leaves to garnish

Tempering
1 tablespoon ghee or oil
1 teaspoon mustard seeds
1 teaspoon cumin seeds
1 dried red chili
pinch of asafoetida powder
4-6 curry leaves

1 Mix the tamarind in 2 cups water and set aside.
2 Wash and cook toor dal in 2-1/2 cups water for 15-20 minutes, until creamy. Mix and set aside with its cooking liquid.
3 Prepare the Tempering. Heat 1 tablespoon ghee in a deep saucepan. Add mustard seeds, cumin seeds, dried red chili, asafoetida powder and curry leaves. Let the mustard seeds splutter.
4 Add the chopped tomatoes, tamarind water, Mysore Rasam Powder, jaggery, turmeric powder and salt to taste. Stir to mix. Simmer for 5-7 minutes over medium heat.
5 Add the cooked dal with its cooking liquid. Simmer for 4-5 minutes over medium heat.
6 Add coconut milk, coriander leaves and heat through for a minute. Serve hot with steamed rice and papaddum.

Mysore Rasam Powder　マイソルラッサムパウダー

材料 100g
お好みの油　大さじ1
コリアンダーシード　大さじ2
黒胡椒　大さじ1
クミンシード　大さじ1
フェヌグリーグシード　大さじ1
カレーリーフ　8〜10枚
鷹の爪　3〜4本

フライパンに油を入れ加熱し、すべての材料を入れる。香りが立つまで、中火で2〜3分炒める。ブレンダーに移し、粉砕する。

Makes 100g
1 tablespoon oil
2 tablespoon coriander seed
1 tablespoon black peppercorn
1 tablespoon cumin seeds
1 teaspoon fenugreek seeds
8-10 curry leaves
3-4 dried red chilies

Heat 1 tablespoon oil in a saucepan. Add all the above ingredients. Saute for 2-3 minutes over medium heat, until fragrant. Transfer to an electric mixer and grind to a powder.

Rasam Vada

Lentil Dumplings in Spicy Tomato Soup　ラッサムワダ

カリッと食感のワダとラッサムスープが合わさった一品。
Crisp Vada in hot Rasam - a delightful blend of texture and flavor.

トマトラッサムにプルップワダ（P81）もしくはメドワダ（P84）を入れ、
中火で5〜7分煮る。コリアンダーリーフをトッピングする。

Rasam Vada with Paruppu Vada：Prepare Tomato Rasam. Follow the recipe for Parrupu Vada on P81. Immerse the Vada into the hot Tomato Rasam. Simmer for 5-7 minutes over medium heat. Garnish with coriander leaves and serve.
Rasam Vada with Medu Vada：Prepare Tomato Rasam. Follow the recipe for Medu Vada on P84. Vada can be made in a doughnut shape or as small dumplings. Immerse the Vada into the hot Tomato Rasam. Simmer for 5-7 minutes over medium heat. Garnish with coriander leaves and serve.

Milagu Rasam -Pepper Rasam-　ペッパーラッサム

インドでは、風邪をひいたときの家庭治療薬としてペッパーラッサムが親しまれています。
A spicy and tangy variety of rasam, considered to be the perfect home remedy for the common cold.

材料　4人分
タマリンドペースト　1・1/2
｜　黒胡椒　小さじ1
A クミンシード　小さじ1
｜　トゥール豆　小さじ1
ラッサムパウダー　小さじ1
塩　適量
テンパリング
ギー　大さじ1
マスタードシード　小さじ1/2
鷹の爪　1本（半分に切る）
アサファティーダパウダー　1つまみ
カレーリーフ　4〜6枚

1　タマリンドペーストを水3カップに溶かす。
2　フライパンにAを入れ、2〜3分煎る。ブレンダーに移し、細かく粉砕する。
3　テンパリングをする。鍋にギーを入れ、材料を加えてパチパチとはじけるまで炒める。
4　1、2、ラッサムパウダー、塩を入れて味をととのえ、中火で3〜4分煮る。

Serves 4
1·1/2 teaspoon tamarind paste
1 teaspoon whole peppercorn
1 teaspoon cumin seeds
1 teaspoon toor dal
1 teaspoon rasam powder
salt to taste
Tempering
1 tablespoon ghee
1/2 teaspoon mustard seeds
1 dried red chili, halved
pinch of asafoetida powder
4-6 curry leaves

1 Mix the tamarind in 3 cups water and set aside.
2 In a saucepan, dry roast the peppercorn, cumin seeds and toor dal for 2-3 minutes. Transfer to an electric mixer and grind to a smooth powder. Set aside.
3 Prepare the Tempering. Heat ghee in a deep saucepan. Add the mustard seeds, dried red chili, asafoetida powder, curry leaves and let the seeds splutter.
4 Add the tamarind water, ground pepper masala, rasam powder and salt to taste. Simmer for 3-4 minutes over medium heat.

Rice and Noodle

ライス＆ヌードル

日本と同じように、米を主食とする南インド。長粒米を使う料理をはじめとして、フォーやビーフンとして知られている"ライスヌードル"が親しまれています。米料理の調理には、スパイスや野菜はもちろん、グリーンピースやカシューナッツなど、アクセントになる食材を加えていただきます。カレーやスープと合わせても、一品でも満足にいただける米料理をご紹介します。レシピには本場の「長粒米」と書いてありますが、日本のお米でも美味しく作ることができます。お好きなお米で試してみてください。

Thakkali Sadam

Tomato Rice　トマトライス

トマトとスパイス、フレッシュなコリアンダーの香り高いトマトライス。お弁当にもおすすめです。

Perfect for a lunch box, steamed long grain rice is tossed in an aromatic mixture of tomato, spices and fresh coriander.

Rice
Noodles

材料　4人分

長粒米　1・1/2カップ
お好みの油　大さじ2
ピーナッツ　大さじ3
玉ねぎ　1個（みじん）
コリアンダーリーフ　適量

マサラベース

お好みの油　小さじ2
ウラド豆　小さじ1
チャナ豆　小さじ1
フェンネルシード　大さじ1
コリアンダーシード　小さじ2
鷹の爪　2本（半分に切る）
ココナッツパウダー　大さじ3

テンパリング

ココナッツオイル　小さじ2
ベイリーフ　1枚
マスタードシード　小さじ1
アサファティーダパウダー　1つまみ
カレーリーフ　6〜8枚

A
トマト　2個（角切り）
生姜　小さじ1（みじん）
チリパウダー　小さじ1
ターメリックパウダー　小さじ1/2
塩　適量

1 長粒米を浸水させ、炊き上がったら冷ましておく。
2 マサラベースを作る。鍋に油を入れ、ココナッツパウダー以外の材料を加えて炒める。ココナッツパウダーを加え混ぜ合わせたら、ミキサーに移し少量の水を足してペースト状にする。
3 別の鍋に油を入れ、ピーナッツをきつね色になるまで炒めたら取り出す。
4 テンパリングをする。3の鍋にココナッツオイルを入れ加熱し、材料を入れてパチパチとはじけるまでかき混ぜながら炒める。さらに玉ねぎを加え、軽く茶色になるまで3〜4分炒める。
5 Aを加え2〜3分炒める。
6 2を加えて混ぜ、1と3を入れ、コリアンダーリーフを少し加えて全体を混ぜる。
7 器に盛り、残りのコリアンダーリーフをトッピングする。揚げたパパドと一緒に食べる。

メモ：フレッシュなトマトが最適ですが、缶詰のトマトでも代用できます。

Serves 4

1・1/2 cups long grain rice
1 tablespoon oil
3 tablespoon peanuts
1 onion, finely chopped
3 tomatoes, chopped
1 teaspoon ginger, finely chopped
1/2 teaspoon turmeric powder
1 teaspoon red chili powder
salt to taste
1/2 cup coriander leaves, chopped

Coconut Masala

1 teaspoon urad dal
1 teaspoon chana dal
2 teaspoon coriander seeds
1 teaspoon fennel seeds
2 dried red chilies, halved
3 tablespoon fresh coconut, grated or powdered coconut

Tempering

2 teaspoon coconut oil
1 bay leaf
1 teaspoon mustard seeds
pinch of asafoatida powder
6-8 curry leaves

1 Cook the rice in 4-5 cups water as per cooking instruction on P15. Drain the rice and return to the saucepan to cool.
2 Prepare the Coconut Masala. Heat a saucepan, add the urad dal, chana dal, coriander seeds, fennel seeds, dried red chilies and dry roast for 2-3 minutes, until the dals change color. Add the coconut and stir to mix. Transfer to an electric mixer and blend to a smooth paste, using a little water. Set aside.
3 Heat 1 tablespoon oil in saucepan, add peanuts and saute for 1-2 minutes. Remove with a slotted spoon and set aside.
4 Prepare the Tempering. To the same pan, add the coconut oil, bay leaf mustard seeds, asafoetida powder and curry leaves. Allow the seeds to splutter. Add chopped onion and saute for 3-4 minutes, until lightly browned.
5 Add chopped tomato, ginger, turmeric powder, red chili powder and salt to taste. Cook for 2-3 minutes.
6 Add the Ground Coconut Masala and mix thoroughly. Stir in the cooked rice, sauteed peanuts and some coriander leaves mix well and heat through.
7 Transfer to a serving dish. Garnish with remaining coriander leaves. Serve with Cucumber and Lentil salad and fried Papaddum.

Memo：Tastes best with fresh tomato, but canned tomato can be a good substitute.

Elumichapazham Sadam

Lemon Rice レモンライス

爽やかな香りが特徴のレモンライスは、タミル・ナドゥー州で親しまれている一品。
Light and tangy with the refreshing flavor of lemon, this easy dish is a Tamil Nadu favorite.

材料　4人分
長粒米　1・1/2カップ
レモン汁　大さじ3
ターメリックパウダー　小さじ1/2
塩　適量
お好みの油　大さじ1
カシューナッツ　大さじ1（半分に割る）
ピーナッツ　大さじ2
青唐辛子　1本（みじん）
アサファティーダパウダー　1つまみ
カレーリーフ　6〜8枚

テンパリング
ゴマ油　小さじ2
マスタードシード　小さじ1
クミンシード　小さじ1
ウラド豆　小さじ1
チャナ豆　小さじ1
鷹の爪　2本（半分に切る）

1　長粒米を浸水させ、炊き上がったら冷ましておく。
2　ボウルにレモン汁、ターメリックパウダー、塩を入れ混ぜ合わせ、1と合わせてやさしくかき混ぜる。
3　フライパンに油を入れ加熱し、カシューナッツとピーナッツを中火で3〜4分炒める。しっかりときつね色になったら取り出す。
4　テンパリングをする。3のフライパンに油を入れ加熱し、材料を加えパチパチとはじけて豆の色が変わるまでかき混ぜながら炒める。
5　青唐辛子、アサファティーダパウダー、カレーリーフを加えて混ぜ合わせたら2と合わせ、2〜3分加熱しながらごはんをつぶさないようにやさしく混ぜる。
6　器に盛りつけ3を添える。

Serves 4
1・1/2 cups long grain rice
1/2 teaspoon turmeric powder
3 tablespoon lemon juice
salt to taste
1 tablespoon oil
1 tablespoon cashews, broken
2 tablespoon peanuts

Tempering
2 teaspoon sesame oil
1 teaspoon mustard seeds
1 teaspoon cumin seeds
1 teaspoon urad dal
1 teaspoon chana dal
2 dried red chilies, halved
1 green chili, finely chopped
pinch of asafoetida powder
6-8 curry leaves

1　Cook the rice as per cooking instructions for steamed rice on P15. Drain the rice and return to the saucepan to cool.
2　In a small bowl, combine lemon juice, turmeric powder and salt. Add this mixture to the cooked rice and toss gently to mix. Set aside.
3　Heat tablespoon oil in saucepan, add the cashews, peanuts and saute for 3-4 minutes on medium heat, until well browned. Remove with a slotted spoon and set aside.
4　Prepare the Tempering. To the same saucepan, add 2 teaspoon sesame oil. Add mustard seeds, cumin seeds, urad dal, chana dal and dried red chilies. Stir briefly over medium heat. until the mustard seeds splutter and the dals turn golden.
5　Add the green chili, asafoetida powder, curry leaves and stir to mix.
6　Add the lemon rice and stir gently so as not to break the rice grains. Cook for 2-3 minutes. Transfer to a serving dish. Garnish with the sauteed cashews, peanuts and serve with Beans Poriyal or Vegetable Pachadi and Papaddum.

Thengai Sadam
Coconut Rice ココナッツライス

シンプルな味つけのココナッツライスは、インドのお祝いの場面で頻繁に食べられている一皿。
Fresh coconut and aromatic curry leaves define this simple yet classic dish, often served on festive occasions.

材料【4人分】
長粒米　1・1/2カップ
お好みの油　大さじ1
カシューナッツ　大さじ2（砕く）
ココナッツシュレッド　1/2カップ
アサファティーダパウダー　1つまみ
カレーリーフ　4〜6枚
塩　適量
テンパリング
お好みの油　大さじ1
マスタードシード　小さじ1
クミンシード　小さじ1
ウラド豆　小さじ1
チャナ豆　小さじ1
鷹の爪　1〜2本

Serves 4
1・1/2 cups long grained rice
1 tablespoon oil
2 tablespoon cashew, broken
1 cup fresh coconut grated or 1/2 cup shredded coconut
salt to taste
Tempering
1 tablespoon oil
1 teaspoon mustard seeds
1 teaspoon cumin seeds
1 teaspoon urad dal
1 teaspoon chana dal
1-2 dried red chilies
pinch of asafoetida powder
4-6 curry leaves

1 長粒米を洗い、水にしばらく浸水させて炊く。
2 フライパンに油を入れ加熱し、カシューナッツを炒める。きつね色になったら取り出す。
3 2と同じフライパンで、ココナッツシュレッドを軽く茶色になるまで炒め、取り出してカシューナッツと一緒にしておく。
4 テンパリングをする。3のフライパンに油を入れ加熱し、材料を加える。マスタードシードをパチパチとはじけさせる。
5 アサファティーダパウダーとカレーリーフを加えて混ぜ合わせる。炊けたごはんと塩を加え、スパイス全体とよく混ぜる。
6 3を加え、ごはんをつぶさないようにやさしく混ぜる。プリアルやパチャディーなどの野菜料理と一緒に食べる。

1 Cook the rice as per cooking instructions on P15. Drain the water and set aside to cool. The grains should be separate.
2 Heat 1 table spoon oil in a saucepan, and saute the cashews until lightly browned. Remove with a slotted spoon and set aside.
3 In the same oil, saute shredded coconut until lightly browned. Remove and set aside.
4 Prepare the Tempering. Heat 1 tablespoon oil in a saucepan, and add mustard seeds, cumin seeds, urad dal, chana dal and dried red chilies. Stir briefly until the mustard seeds splutter and the dals get lightly browned.
5 Add asafoetida powder, curry leaves and stir. Add the cooked rice and salt to taste. Mix well to combine with the spices.
6 Stir in the roasted coconut, sauteed cashews and mix gently, heat through and serve hot with vegetable dish such as Cabbage Poriyal, Beans Poriyal or Bitter Gourd Pachadi.

Pattani Sadam

Green Peas Rice　グリーンピースライス

どんな料理とも合うシンプルなごはん。ヨーグルトサラダと合わせて。
A simple, delicious rice dish perfect for every occasion, be it a lazy weekend or a festive party.

材料　4人分

長粒米　1カップ
玉ねぎ　1個（みじん）
ミント　1/4カップ
  人参　1/2本（みじん）
  グリーンピース　1カップ
A ターメリックパウダー　小さじ1/2
  塩　適量

マサラベース

お好みの油　小さじ2
ウラド豆　大さじ2
チャナ豆　大さじ2
コリアンダーシード　大さじ2
鷹の爪　2〜3本
アサファティーダパウダー　1つまみ

テンパリング

お好みの油　大さじ1
ベイリーフ　2枚
シナモンスティック　小1本
クローブ　2〜3粒
黒胡椒　6〜8粒
クミンシード　小さじ1/2
鷹の爪　2本（半分に切る）
カレーリーフ　4〜6枚

1 長粒米を洗い、水にしばらく浸水させて炊く。
2 マサラベースを作る。フライパンに油を入れて、ウラド豆とチャナ豆を加え、色が変わるまで軽く炒めたら、残りの材料を加え、香りが立ったら火からおろす。
3 2をブレンダーで粉砕する。
4 テンパリングをする。フライパンに油を入れ加熱し、材料を入れパチパチとはじけ豆の色が変わるまでかき混ぜながら炒める。
5 玉ねぎを加え3〜4分炒めたらAを加え、野菜がやわらかくなるまで5〜6分中火にかける。
6 3を入れ静かにかき混ぜ、1とミントを加えて2〜3分加熱する。全粒粉パンやパパドと一緒に食べる。

Serves 4

1·1/2 cup long grain rice
1 onion, chopped
1 cup shelled green peas
1/2 carrot, peeled and chopped
1/4 cup mint leaves, chopped
1/2 teaspoon turmeric powder
salt to taste

Ground Masala

2 teaspoon oil
1 teaspoon urad dal
1 teaspoon chana dal
2 teaspoon coriander seeds
2-3 dried red chilies
pinch of asafoetida powder

Tempering

1 tablespoon oil
2 bay leaves
1 small stick cinnamon
1/2 teaspoon cumin seeds
2 dried red chilies, halved
4-6 curry leaves

1 Cook the rice as per cooking instructions on P15. Drain the water and set aside to cool. The grains should be separate.
2 Prepare the Ground Masala. Heat oil in a saucepan, add urad dal, chana dal and stir briefly until the dals change color. Add coriander seeds, dried red chilies and asafoetida powder. Stir briefly and remove from heat.
3 Place in an electric mixer and grind to a fine powder. Set aside.
4 Prepare the Tempering. Heat oil in a saucepan, and bay leaves, cinnamon stick and stir briefly. Add cumin seeds, dried red chilies, curry leaves and stir briefly.
5 Add chopped onion and saute for 3-4 minutes. Add carrots, green peas and mix. Add turmeric powder and salt to taste. Add a little water and cook covered over medium heat for 5-6 minutes, until the vegetables are tender.
6 Add the ground masala to the vegetables and mix well.
7 Add the mint leaves, cooked rice and toss gently to mix. Taste for salt. Cook for 2-3 minutes and serve with Okra Pachadi or Bittergourd Pachadi and some fried papaddum.

Bisi Bele Huli Anna

Spicy Rice from Karnataka　スパイシーピラフ

お祝いの場面で登場するスパイシーピラフ。タマリンドソースが奥深い味わいを生み出します。

No celebration in Karnataka is complete without this traditional recipe of rice and lentils cooked together in spicy tamarind sauce.

材料　4人分

長粒米　1カップ
トゥール豆　3/4カップ
お好みの油　大さじ2
玉ねぎ　1個（みじん）
人参　1本（みじん）
インゲン豆　4〜6本（2cm）
グリーンピース　1/2カップ（ゆで）

A
| ベビーオニオン　6〜8個
| トマト　2個（角切り）
| ターメリックパウダー　小さじ1/2
| タマリンドペースト　小さじ1（水1/4カップに溶かす）
| 黒糖　小さじ1
| 塩　適量

マサラ

コリアンダーシード　大さじ1・1/2
チャナ豆　大さじ1
ウラド豆　大さじ1/2
鷹の爪　4本
クミンシード　小さじ1/2
フェヌグリーグシード　小さじ1/2
クローブ　2〜3粒
黒胡椒　10〜12粒
ココナッツパウダー　大さじ1

テンパリング

ギー　大さじ2
カシューナッツ　6〜7粒（砕く）
マスタードシード　小さじ1/2
鷹の爪　1本
アサファティーダパウダー　1つまみ
カレーリーフ　4〜6枚

1 長粒米とトゥール豆を合わせて洗い30分浸水させ、ザルにあけておく。
2 マサラを作る。加熱したフライパンにココナッツパウダー以外の材料を入れ、中火で1〜2分炒める。豆に色がついたらココナッツパウダーを加えて混ぜ、ブレンダーに移し撹拌する。
3 大きめの鍋に油大さじ2を入れ加熱し、玉ねぎを2〜3分炒める。そこにAを加え、全体をよく混ぜ合わせる。
4 人参、インゲン豆、グリーンピースを加え、塩で味をととのえる。
5 1、2、水4カップを加えて、よく混ぜてから炊飯器に入れ、やわらかくクリーミーになるまで炊いたらフライパンに移して混ぜる。
6 テンパリングをする。別のフライパンにギーを入れ加熱し、カシューナッツを1〜2分炒める。きつね色になったら取り出し、同じフライパンに残りの材料を入れ、パチパチとはじけるまでかき混ぜながら炒める。
7 炊き上がったごはんの上にカシューナッツとテンパリングをかけて完成。パパドやヨーグルトサラダと食べる。

メモ：ギーを使用することで、風味豊かなスパイシーピラフができあがります。

Memo : Ghee lends an added richness to the dish.

Serves 4

1 cup long grain rice
3/4 cup toor dal
1 carrot, peeled and cut into small pieces
4-6 beans, cut into 2 cm pieces
1/2 cup green peas, shelled
2 tablespoon oil
1 onion, chopped
6-8 shallots or baby onions, peeled
2 tomatoes, chopped
1/2 teaspoon turmeric powder
1 teaspoon tamarind pulp
1 teaspoon jaggery
salt to taste

Bisi Bela Masala

1 · 1/2 tablespoon coriander seeds
1 tablespoon chana dal
1/2 tablespoon urad dal
4 dried red chilies
1/2 teaspoon cumin seeds
1/2 teaspoon fenugreek seeds
10-11 black peppercorn
2-3 cloves
1 table spoon fresh grated coconut or powdered coconut

Tempering

2 tablespoon ghee
6-7 cashews, broken
1/2 teaspoon mustard seeds
1 dried red chili, halved
pinch of asafoetida powder
4-6 curry leaves

1 Wash and soak the toor dal and rice together in water for 30 minutes. Drain the water and set aside. Dissolve the tamarind pulp in 1/4 cup water and set aside.
2 Prepare the Bisi Bela Masala. Heat a saucepan and place coriander seeds, chana dal, urad dal, dried red chilies, cumin seeds, fenugreek seeds, whole peppercorns, cinnamon and cloves. Dry roast over medium heat for 1-2 minutes. Keep stirring until the dals change color. Add the grated coconut and mix. Remove from heat and transfer to an electric mixer. Grind to a smooth powder and set aside.
3 To Proceed Heat 2 tablespoon oil in a large saucepan, saute the onions for 2-3 minutes until translucent. Add shallots, and stir briefly. Add tomatoes, turmeric powder, tamarind extract, jaggery and stir to mix.
4 Add the carrot, beans, peas and mix. Add salt to taste. Add the ground Bisi Bela Masala and mix well. Add the drained rice and dal mixture and saute briefly. Add 4 cups water and salt to taste. Transfer to a rice cooker and cook until soft and creamy.
5 Once cooked, transfer to a saucepan and mix lightly with a spoon.
6 Prepare the Tempering. Heat 2 tablespoon ghee in a skillet, and saute the cashews for 1-2 minutes, until light brown. Remove with a slotted spoon and set aside. Add mustard seeds, dried red chili, asafoetida powder, curry leaves and allow the seeds to splutter. Pour over the lentil and rice mixture and mix well.
7 Transfer to a serving dish. Garnish with sauteed cashews and serve with Vegetable Yogurt Salad, and Papaddum.

Ven Pongal

Rice and Lentil Risotto 豆とスパイスのリゾット

お米とムング豆で調理するリゾットは、朝食にもおすすめ。ギーをかけるとより美味しくなります。

Rice and yellow Moong dal combined with whole spices and a dollop of ghee make for a rich weekend breakfast.

材料　4人分

長粒米　1カップ

ムング豆（緑または黄）　1/2カップ

カシューナッツ　大さじ2（砕く）

塩　適量

マサラ

ギー　大さじ2

クミンシード　小さじ1/2

黒胡椒　小さじ1/2（つぶす）

青唐辛子　2本（スライス）

生姜　大さじ1（みじん）

アサファティーダパウダー　1つまみ

カレーリーフ　6〜8枚

1　フライパンを熱し、長粒米とムング豆をそれぞれ中火で数分炒めておく。

2　1をそれぞれよく洗い、しばらく浸水させる。鍋に水4カップを入れて沸騰させたところに米を加え、時々かき混ぜながら中火で15〜18分加熱する。さらにやわらかくとろりとするまで10〜12分弱火にかける（炊飯器または圧力鍋を使用してもOK）。

3　フライパンに油を入れ、カシューナッツをきつね色になるまで炒め、取り出す。

4　マサラを作る。3のフライパンに材料を加え、かき混ぜながら炒める。

5　炊き上がった長粒米とムング豆を加え、塩で味をととのえる。少量の水でお好みのやわらかさにして、弱火にしてやさしく混ぜる。

6　3とギーをトッピングする。ベビーオニオンサンバルまたはカリフラワーサンバル、ココナッツチャツネと食べる。

メモ：ギーをかけることで、最高の味になります。

Serves 4

1 cup long grain rice

1/2 cup yellow / dal or green moong dal

2 tablespoon cashews, broken

salt to taste

Masala

2 tablespoon ghee

1/2 teaspoon whole peppercorns

1/2 teaspoon cumin seeds

2 green chilies, slit

1 tablespoon ginger, finely chopped

pinch of asafoetida powder

6-8 curry leaves

1　In a large saucepan, dry roast moong dal over medium heat for a few minutes. Set aside.

2　Wash the rice and moong dal, and place together in a large saucepan. Add 3·1/2cups water and a dash of salt. Transfer to a rice cooker and cook until soft and creamy.

3　Heat 2 tablespoon ghee in a saucepan, and saute the cashews for a few minutes, until golden brown. Remove with a slotted and set aside.

4　Prepare the Masala. To the same pan, add cumin seeds, whole peppercorns, green chilies, ginger, asafoetida powder, curry leaves and saute for a minute.

5　Add the cooked rice and dal mixture and adjust the salt to taste. Add a little water if the mixture seems bit dry. Mix gently over low heat.

6　Garnish with sauteed cashews and top with a little ghee. Serve hot with Baby Onion Sambar or Cauliflower Sambar and Coconut Chutney.

Memo：Tastes best topped with ghee.

Thengai Sevaii

Coconut Rice Noodles ココナッツライスヌードル

南インドの最もおいしいライスヌードルの料理。お好みのチャツネと一緒に。朝食にもおすすめ。
One of the tastiest yet simplest South Indian dishes, served with tomato chutney. Perfect for breakfast.

材料　4人分
ライスヌードル　100g（砕く）
お好みの油　大さじ1
カシューナッツ　小さじ1（砕く）
ピーナッツ　小さじ1
玉ねぎ　1個（みじん）
ココナッツパウダー　1/2カップ
塩　適量
テンパリング
ゴマ油　大さじ1
マスタードシード　小さじ1
チャナ豆　小さじ1
ウラド豆　小さじ1
鷹の爪　2本
青唐辛子　1本（みじん）
アサファティーダパウダー　1つまみ
カレーリーフ　4〜6枚

1 鍋にたっぷりの水を沸騰させ、ライスヌードルを入れる。
  1分後火を止め、フタをして3〜4分蒸らしたらザルにあ
  け器に移して冷ます。
2 フライパンに油を入れ、カシューナッツとピーナッツを
  1〜2分炒め、きつね色になったら取り出す。
3 テンパリングをする。2のフライパンに材料を入れ加熱
  し、パチパチとはじけるまでかき混ぜる。
4 玉ねぎを加え3〜4分炒め、軽く茶色になったら、ココ
  ナッツパウダーを入れ、再び1分ほど炒める。
5 1、2、塩を入れ、弱火で2〜3分かき混ぜながら加熱する。
  ココナッツチャツネと食べる。

Serves 4
2 cups rice noodles / vermicelli, broken into small pieces
1 tablespoon oil
1 teaspoon cashews, broken
1 teaspoon peanuts
1 onion, finely chopped
1/2 cup grated coconut or powdered coconut
salt to taste
Tempering
1 tablespoon sesame oil
1 teaspoon mustard seeds
1 teaspoon chana dal
1 teaspoon urad dal
2 dried red chilies
1 green chili, finely chopped
1/4 teaspoon asafoetida powder
4-6 curry leaves

1 Bring 4 cups of water to a boil, in a saucepan. Add the rice
  noodles and cook for a minute. Turn off the heat and keep
  covered for 3-4 minutes. Drain the water and transfer to a dish
  to cool.
2 Heat the oil in a saucepan, saute the cashews and peanuts for
  1-2 minutes, until lightly browned. Remove with a slotted spoon
  and set aside.
3 Prepare the Tempering. To the same saucepan, add sesame oil,
  mustard seeds, urad and chana dal, dried red chilies, green
  chilies, asafoetida powder and curry leaves. Saute lightly until
  the mustard seeds splutter.
4 Add the chopped onions and saute for 3-4 minutes, until
  translucent. Add the grated coconut and saute for a minute,
  over medium heat until lightly browned.
5 Add the cooked rice noodles, sauteed cashews and peanuts.
  Add salt to taste. Mix thoroughly and cook on low heat for 2-3
  minutes. Serve with Tomato Chutney.

Thakkali Sevaii

Tomato Rice Noodles　トマトライスヌードル

フレッシュなトマトとコリアンダーリーフを使えば、カラフルでおいしいライスヌードルに。
Tangy and colorful. Fresh tomato and coriander leaves add a delightful flavor to this healthy breakfast noodle dish.

材料　4人分
ライスヌードル　100g（砕く）
お好みの油　大さじ1
カシューナッツ　大さじ1（砕く）
ピーナッツ　大さじ1
玉ねぎ　1個（みじん）
人参　大さじ3
トマト　2個
生姜　大さじ1（みじん）
サンバルパウダー　小さじ1
ターメリックパウダー　小さじ1/2
塩　適量
コリアンダーリーフ　適量

テンパリング
ゴマ油　大さじ1
マスタードシード　小さじ1
クミンシード　小さじ1/2
ウラド豆　小さじ1
アサファティーダパウダー　1つまみ
カレーリーフ　4〜6枚

1 鍋にたっぷりの水を沸騰させ、ライスヌードルを入れる。1分後火を止め、フタをして3〜4分蒸らしたらザルにあけ器に移して冷ます。
2 フライパンに油を入れ、カシューナッツとピーナッツを1〜2分炒め、きつね色になったら取り出す。
3 テンパリングをする。2のフライパンに材料を入れ加熱し、パチパチはじけ、豆の色が変わるまでかき混ぜながら炒める。
4 玉ねぎを加え、軽く茶色くなるまで中火で1〜2分炒める。
5 人参、トマト、生姜、サンバルパウダー、ターメリックパウダー、塩を加えよく混ぜる。トマトがやわらかくなるまで加熱する。
6 1と2を加え、弱火で2〜3分混ぜながら炒める。コリアンダーリーフをかける。ココナッツチャツネと一緒に食べる。

バリエーション：玉ねぎとムング豆、人参、インゲン豆を加え、2〜3分炒めたものを加えると、ベジタブルライスヌードルになります。

Serves 4
2cups rice noodles / vermicelli, broken into small pieces
1 onion, finely chopped
2 tomatoes, chopped
1 tablespoon ginger, finely chopped
1 teaspoon sambar powder
1/2 teaspoon turmeric powder
salt to taste
1 tablespoon oil
1 tablespoon peanuts
1 tablespoon cashews, broken
coriander leaves to garnish

Tempering
1 tablespoon sesame oil
1 teaspoon mustard seeds
1/2 teaspoon cumin seeds
1 teaspoon urad dal
1-2 dried red chilies
1 green chili, finely chopped
pinch of asafoetida powder
4-6 curry leaves

1 In a saucepan, bring 4 cups of water to a boil. Add the rice noodles and cook for a minute. Turn off the heat and keep covered for 3-4 minutes. Drain the water and transfer to a dish to cool.
2 Heat the oil in a saucepan, and saute the cashews and peanuts for 1-2 minutes, until lightly browned. Remove with a slotted spoon and set aside.
3 Prepare the Tempering. To the same saucepan, add the sesame oil, mustard seeds, cumin seeds, urad dal dried red chilies, green chilies, asafoetida powder and curry leaves. Saute lightly until the mustard seeds splutter and the urad dal turns golden.
4 Add chopped onion and saute for 1-2 minutes, over medium heat until lightly browned.
5 Add tomatoes, ginger, sambar powder, turmeric powder and salt to taste. Mix well and cook for 2-3 minutes, until tomatoes turn soft.
6 Add the cooked rice noodles, sauteed cashews, peanuts and mix thoroughly. Cook on low heat for 2-3 minutes. Serve with Coconut Chutney.

Variation: For Vegetable Sevai. Add chopped green beans, carrots and peas to the onions and saute for 2-3 minutes. Follow the same recipe as above.

Elumichapazham Sevai

Lemon Rice Noodles　レモンライスヌードル

タミル・ナドゥ一州で人気のライスヌードル。スパイシーな味わいはティフィンと合わせても。
Especially popular in Tamil Nadu, these tangy and spicy noodles are a Tiffin favorite.

材料　4人分

ライスヌードル　100g
お好みの油　大さじ1
カシューナッツ　大さじ2（砕く）
ピーナッツ　大さじ2
塩　適量
レモン汁　大さじ2

テンパリング

ゴマ油　大さじ1
マスタードシード　小さじ1
ウラド豆　大さじ1
チャナ豆　大さじ1
クミンシード　小さじ1
カレーリーフ　6〜8枚

A |　玉ねぎ　1個（みじん）
|　青唐辛子　2本（みじん）
|　生姜　小さじ1（みじん）
|　ターメリックパウダー　小さじ1/4

1 鍋にたっぷりの水を沸騰させ、ライスヌードルを入れる。1分後火を止め、フタをして3〜4分蒸らしたらザルにあけ器に移して冷ます。
2 フライパンに油を入れ、カシューナッツとピーナッツを1〜2分炒め、きつね色になったら取り出す。
3 テンパリングをする。2のフライパンに油を入れ加熱し、材料を加え、パチパチはじけて豆の色が変わるまでかき混ぜながら炒める。
4 Aを加え、かき混ぜながら3〜4分加熱し、1と塩を加える。
5 2とレモン汁を加え、弱火で2〜3分混ぜながら煮る。
6 器に盛り、ココナッツチャツネと一緒に食べる。

Serves 4

2cups dried rice noodles / vermicelli, broken into small pieces
1 tablespoon oil
2 tablespoon cashews, broken
1 onion, finely chopped
2 green chilies, finely chopped
1 teaspoon ginger, finely chopped
1/4 teaspoon turmeric powder
2 tablespoon fresh lemon juice
2 tablespoon peanuts
salt to taste

Tempering

1 tablespoon sesame oil
1 teaspoon mustard seeds
1 teaspoon cumin seeds
1 tablespoon urad dal
1 tablespoon chana dal
6 curry leaves

1 In a saucepan, bring 4 cups of water to a boil. Add the rice noodles and cook for a minute. Turn off the heat and keep covered for 3-4 minutes. Drain the water and transfer to a dish to cool.
2 Heat the oil in a saucepan, saute the cashews and peanuts for 1-2 minutes, until lightly browned. Remove with a slotted spoon and set aside.
3 Prepare the Tempering. To the same saucepan, add the sesame oil, and return to heat. Add mustard seeds, cumin seeds, urad dal, chana dal and curry leaves. Saute lightly over medium heat, until the mustard seeds splutter and the dals turn golden.
4 Add the onions, green chilies, ginger and saute for 3-4 minutes. Stir in the cooked rice noodles. Add turmeric powder, salt to taste, lemon juice and mix thoroughly.
5 Add the sauteed cashews, peanuts and cook for 2-3 minutes, until the flavors are well blended. Serve warm with Coconut Chutney.

——— Home Remedy ———

ノドの不調に

For relief from sore throat

Turmeric Milk　ターメリックミルク

フライパンに牛乳1カップを入れ加熱し、水1/4、塩1つまみ、ターメリック小さじ1を入れ、2〜3分煮る。塩の代わりにハチミツを入れれば、ターメリックハニーミルクに。
Turmeric Milk with Salt : In a saucepan, bring 1 cup milk to a boil. Add 1/4 cup water, dash of salt, 1 teaspoon turmeric powder. Simmer for 2-3 minutes. Pour in a cup and drink while warm.
Turmeric Milk with Honey : Use honey instead of salt to make sweet turmeric milk.

Vegetable and Salad

ベジタブル＆サラダ

日本料理と同じように、インドにも野菜をメインとしたサラダ
や炒め物があります。テンパリングをかけたり、ヨーグルトと
和えたり、炒めたり、さまざまな調理法と組み合わせがありま
すが、どれもこはんやパンとよく合うサイドティッシュです。
細かくて食べやすく、簡単な調理ばかりなので、パーティーメ
ニューにも。ジャンル問わず、お好きなお料理と合わせて召し
上がってみてください。

Kaikari Pacha Paruppu Poriyal

Stir Fried Vegetables with Green Lentils 豆と野菜のポリヤル

カラフルな野菜とココナッツマサラ、ムング豆を合わせたオリジナルの一品。
A colorful stir-fry of vegetables and moong dal tossed in coconut masala paste.

材料　4人分
ムング豆　1/4カップ（スプリット）
人参　1/2本（角切り）
インゲン豆　10〜12本（2cm大）
グリーンピース　1/2カップ
塩　適量
ターメリックパウダー　小さじ1/2
カシューナッツ　適量（揚げる）

マサラペースト
お好みの油　小さじ1
クミンシード　小さじ1/2
黒胡椒　小さじ1
鷹の爪　2本（半分に切る）
ココナッツパウダー　大さじ2

テンパリング
お好みの油　小さじ2
マスタードシード　小さじ1
ウラド豆　小さじ1
鷹の爪　1本
カレーリーフ　4〜6枚

1　ムング豆を1カップの水に30分浸水し、水気を切り鍋に入れる。2カップの水を加え8〜10分間加熱し、やわらかくなったらザルにあけておく。

2　マサラペーストを作る。フライパンに油を入れ加熱し、クミンシード、黒胡椒、鷹の爪を加えてかき混ぜる。さらに、ココナッツパウダーを加えて香りがなくなるまで1分かき混ぜながら加熱する。火からおろし、少量の水とブレンダーで撹拌して細かいペースト状にする。

3　野菜を準備する。人参、インゲン豆、グリーンピースを鍋に入れ、ひたひたになるくらいの水を加える。塩、ターメリックパウダーを加えて4〜5分加熱する。

4　3に1と2を加え、中火で2〜3分加熱し、かき混ぜながら全体の味をなじませる。

5　テンパリングをする。フライパンに油を入れ加熱し、材料を加えパチパチとはじけ、豆の色が変わるまでかき混ぜながら炒める。

6　4に5をかける。スパイシーピラフまたはごはんを使用する場合は、カシューナッツをふりかけてもOK。

メモ：緑ムング豆でも黄ムング豆でも美味しくできます。

Serves 4
1/4 cup green moong dal
1/2 carrot, peeled, chopped
10-12 green beans, cut into 2cm pieces
1/2 cup green peas, shelled
salt to taste
1/2 teaspoon turmeric powder
fried cashews to garnish

Masala Paste
1 teaspoon oil
1/2 teaspoon cumin seeds
1 teaspoon black peppercorns
2 dried red chilies, halved
2 tablespoon fresh coconut grated or powdered coconut

Tempering
2 teaspoon oil
1 teaspoon mustard seeds
1 teaspoon urad dal
1 dried red chili
4-6 curry leaves

1　Wash and soak the moong dal in 1 cup water for 10 minutes. Drain and transfer to a saucepan. Add 2 cups water and cook for 8-10 minutes, until soft. Drain and set aside.

2　Prepare the Masala Paste. Heat 1 teaspoon oil in a saucepan, and add cumin seeds, whole peppercorns, dried red chilies, and stir briefly. Add coconut powder and stir for a minute, until fragrant. Remove from heat and transfer to an electric mixer. Blend to a fine paste, using a little water.

3　Prepare the Vegetables. Place the carrot, beans and peas in a saucepan. Add enough water to cover the vegetables. Add salt to taste, turmeric powder and cook covered for 4-5 minutes, until the vegetables are tender.

4　Add the Masala Paste and cooked moong dal to the vegetables. Mix thoroughly and cook for 2-3 minutes over medium heat to allow the spices to blend.

5　Prepare the Tempering. Heat 2 teaspoon oil in a saucepan. Add mustard seeds, urad dal, dried red chili and curry leaves. When the mustard seeds splutter and the dal changes color, pour the tempering over the vegetable and dal mixture and toss gently to mix.

6　Garnish with fried cashews and serve with Bisi Bela Rice or plain rice.

Memo：Use yellow moong dal instead of green moong dal and follow the recipe as above.

Beans Parupu Usili

Stir-fried Green Beans and Bengal Gram

ビーンズウシリ（インゲン豆のスパイス炒め）

インゲン豆をクリスピーなチャナ豆とミックスした野菜炒め。
Green beans tossed with a crispy chana dal mixture and nutty seasoning.

材料　4人分
チャナ豆　3/4カップ
鷹の爪　2本
アサファティーダパウダー　1つまみ
塩　適量
インゲン豆　300g（みじん）

テンパリング
お好みの油　大さじ1・1/2
マスタードシード　小さじ1
クミンシード　小さじ1/2
鷹の爪　1本（半分に切る）
カレーリーフ　6〜8枚

1 チャナ豆をたっぷりの水に30分浸水させ、水を切る。鍋に移し2カップの水を入れ、半分ほど火が通るまで10〜12分炊く。水を切り、鷹の爪と一緒にブレンダーに入れ、粗い粒になるまで撹拌する。
2 ボウルに1、アサファティーダパウダー、塩を入れて混ぜる。
3 鍋にインゲン豆を入れ、ひたひたになるくらいの水と塩を加え、3〜4分加熱しやわらかくなったら水を切る。
4 テンパリングをする。フライパンに油を入れ加熱し、材料を入れる。パチパチとはじけるまでかき混ぜながら炒める。
5 2を加え、中火で4〜5分加熱する。3を加えて2〜3分加熱し、よく混ぜる。サンバルやごはんを添えて食べる。

Serves 4
3/4 cup chana dal
2 dried red chilies
pinch of asafoetida powder
salt to taste
300g green beans, finely chopped

Tempering
1・1/2 tablespoon oil
1 teaspoon mustard seeds
1/2 teaspoon cumin seeds
1 dried red chili, halved
6-8 curry leaves

1 Soak the chana dal in 2 cups water for 30 minutes. Drain and transfer to a saucepan. Add 2 cups water and cook for 10-12 minutes, until half done. Drain the water and place in an electric mixer. Add dried red chilies and grind to a coarse mix.
2 Transfer to a bowl. Add salt to taste and asafoetida powder. Mix and set aside.
3 In a another saucepan, place the green beans, and add enough water to cover. Add salt to taste and cook for 3-4 minutes, until tender. Drain and set aside.
4 Prepare the Tempering. Heat 1・1/2 tablespoon oil in a saucepan, add mustard seeds, cumin seeds, dried red chili and curry leaves. Stir briefly until the mustard seeds splutter.
5 Add the ground chana dal mixture and stir to mix. Cook covered for 4-5 minutes over medium heat, until the mixture crumbly in texture. Stir in the cooked green beans, mix well and cook for 2-3 minutes, over medium heat.
Serve with sambar and rice to make a complete meal.

Vegetable Salad

Muttaikkos Poriyal

Stir fried Cabbage with Grated Coconut

キャベツポリヤル（キャベツのスパイス炒め）

米料理とサンバルと相性のいいキャベツ炒め。簡単で食感が楽しい料理です。
Poriyal is a quick and crunchy accompaniment to rice and sambar.

材料　4人分
キャベツ　250g（みじん）
生姜　小さじ1（みじん）
青唐辛子　1本（みじん）
塩　適量
ココナッツパウダー　大さじ2
ココナッツシュレッド　適量

テンパリング
お好みの油　大さじ1
マスタードシード　小さじ1
ウラド豆　小さじ1
鷹の爪　1本（半分に切る）
アサファティーダパウダー　小さじ1/4
カレーリーフ　6〜8枚

1 テンパリングをする。フライパンに油を入れ加熱し、材料を加える。パチパチはじけ、豆の色が茶色になるまでかき混ぜながら炒める。
2 キャベツ、生姜、青唐辛子を加えよくかき混ぜ、塩で味をととのえる。少量の水を加えて、フタをしてやわらかくなるまで3〜4分弱火で加熱する。
3 ココナッツパウダーを加えかき混ぜたら、さらに1分ほど加熱し、器に盛る。仕上げにココナッツシュレッドを飾り、パラタやごはんと一緒に食べる。

メモ：キャベツ以外のお好みの野菜でもポリヤルができます。

バリエーション：グリーンピースと粗くすりおろした人参を加えてもOK。

Serves 4
250g cabbage, finely chopped
1 teaspoon ginger, finely chopped
1 green chili, chopped
salt to taste
2 tablespoon grated fresh coconut or powdered coconut
shredded coconut or coriander leaves to garnish

Tempering
1 tablespoon oil
1 teaspoon mustard seeds
1 teaspoon urad dal
1 dried red chili, halved
pinch of asafoetida powder
6-8 curry leaves

1 Prepare the Tempering. Heat oil in a saucepan. Add mustard seeds and allow them to splutter. Add urad dal, dried red chili, asafoetida powder and curry leaves. Stir briefly until the dal turns light brown.
2 Add the chopped cabbage, ginger and green chilies. Stir well and add salt to taste. Add a splash of water. Cover and cook over medium low heat for 3-4 minutes until the cabbage is tender.
3 Stir in the grated coconut and cook for another minute. Garnish with coriander leaves or shredded coconut.
Serve with Paratha or rice.

Memo：Freshly grated coconut or coconut powder may be added to any stir- fried vegetable dish to make it a Poriyal.

Variation：Carrot Poriyal or Green Beans Poriyal can be made in the same way.

Kadalai Sundal

Tempered Chick Peas with Coconut　スンダル（ひよこ豆のスパイス炒め）

インドの寺院でも提供されている豆料理。サラダやスナックとして、ヘルシーで風味豊かな味わいです。
Healthy and flavorful, Sundal can be served as a salad or a snack. It is also made as a temple offering at festivals.

材料　4人分

ひよこ豆　200g（ホール）
（水煮の場合　400g）
塩　適量
青唐辛子　2本（みじん）
ココナッツパウダー　大さじ2
ココナッツシュレッド　適量

テンパリング

お好みの油　小さじ2
マスタードシード　小さじ1
ウラド豆　小さじ1
鷹の爪　1本（半分に切る）
アサファティーダパウダー　小さじ1/4
カレーリーフ　4〜6枚

1 ひよこ豆を大きめのボウルに入れ、4〜5カップの水で6〜8時間浸水する。水を切り鍋に入れ、たっぷりの水と塩を入れて30〜40分茹でる。やわらかくなったらザルにあげておく。

2 テンパリングをする。フライパンに油を入れ加熱し、材料を入れパチパチとはじけ、豆の色が変わるまでかき混ぜながら炒める。

3 2に1、青唐辛子、ココナッツパウダーを加えて混ぜ、塩で味をととのえたら火からおろし、器に盛る。

4 ココナッツシュレッドをかける。サラダやスナックとして食べる。

メモ：水煮のひよこ豆を使用する場合は、流水ですすいでから使用する。
茶色ひよこ豆、ムング豆、ピーナッツ、チャナ豆を使用してもOK。

Serves 4

200g dried chick peas or 400g canned chickpeas
2 green chilies, finely chopped
2 tablespoon coconut freshly grated or powdered coconut
salt to taste
shredded coconut to garnish

Tempering

2 teaspoon oil
1 teaspoon mustard seeds
1 teaspoon urad dal
1 dried red chili, halved
pinch of asafoetida powder
curry leaves

1 Place the chick peas in a deep bowl and cover with 4-5 cups water. Soak for 6-8 hours. Drain the liquid and place in a saucepan with 4-5 cups of water. Add ¼ teaspoon salt, and cook for 30-40 minutes on medium heat, until soft. Drain and set aside.

2 Prepare the Tempering. Heat 2 teaspoon oil in a saucepan. Add mustard seeds, urad dal, dried red chili, asafoetida powder, curry leaves. Allow the mustard seeds to splutter and the dal to turn golden.

3 Add the cooked chick peas, green chilies and grated coconut. Add salt to taste and mix thoroughly. Remove from heat.

4 Garnish with shredded coconut and serve as a salad or a snack.

Memo : If using canned chick peas, rinse them under running water.
Sundal can be prepared with brown chick peas, dried peas, mung beans, peanuts and chana dal.

--- Home Remedy ---

寒気を感じたときに
For relief from feeling cold

Coriander Seeds and Peppercorn Drink
コリアンダーシード&黒胡椒のドリンク

フライパンで水2カップを沸騰させ、コリアンダーシード小さじ1、黒胡椒小さじ1/2、黒糖小さじ1を加え、3〜4分煮る。濾してグラスに注ぎ、一日に何度か飲む。

In a saucepan, bring 2 cups of water to a boil. Add 1 teaspoon coriander seeds, 1/2 teaspoon whole black peppercorn, 1 teaspoon jaggery, and simmer for 3-4 minutes. Strain and pour into a glass. Have a few sips from it, through the day.

Vellarikkai Thakkali
Vengaya Pachadi

Vegetable Raita
野菜のヨーグルトサラダ

ケララ州とタミル・ナドゥー州でよく食べられているヨーグルトベースのサラダ。
In Kerala and Tamil Nadu, pachadi is a yogurt-based side dish similar to
the North Indian raita. A soothing side dish to accompany a meal.

Vendakai Tayir Pachadi

Fried Okra with Yogurt

オクラのヨーグルトサラダ

Vegetable Salad

Pavakka Kichadi

Bittergourd Yogurt Salad

ゴーヤーのヨーグルトサラダ

Vellarikkai Thakkali Vengaya Pachadi

Vegetable Yogurt Salad 野菜のヨーグルトサラダ

材料　4人分
ヨーグルト　1・1/2カップ
塩　適量
コリアンダーリーフ
ミント
| キュウリ　1本
| 玉ねぎ　小1個
| トマト　1個
A| 人参　1本
| 青唐辛子　1本
| 生姜　小さじ1

テンパリング
お好みの油　小さじ2
マスタードシード　小さじ1/2
クミンシード　小さじ1/2
ウラド豆　小さじ1/2
アサファティーダパウダー　1つまみ
鷹の爪　1本（半分に切る）
カレーリーフ　4〜6枚

1 Aの野菜をすべて細かいみじん切りにする。玉ねぎ、人参は皮をむいてからみじん切りにする。
2 深めのボウルにヨーグルトを入れ、1と塩を加えて混ぜる。
3 テンパリングをする。フライパンに油を入れ加熱し、材料を入れる。パチパチはじけて香りが立つまでかき混ぜながら炒める。
4 2の上に3を注ぎ、冷やしてからコリアンダーリーフとミントをトッピングして食べる。

メモ：コリアンダーリーフまたはミントをみじん切りして野菜と混ぜるとより美味しくなります。

Serves 4
300g yogurt
1 cucumber, finely chopped
1 small onion, finely chopped
1 tomato, finely chopped
1 tablespoon carrot, finely chopped
1 green chili, finely chopped
1 teaspoon ginger, finely chopped
salt to taste

Tempering
2 teaspoon oil
1/2 teaspoon mustard seeds
1/2 teaspoon cumin seeds
1/2 teaspoon urad dal
pinch of asafoetida powder
1 dried red chili, halved
4-6 curry leaves

1 Prepare all the vegetables and set aside.
2 Place the yogurt in a bowl. Add the finely chopped cucumber, onion, tomato, carrot, green chili, ginger, and salt to taste. Mix well and transfer to a serving dish.
3 Prepare the Tempering. Heat 2 teaspoon oil in a skillet. Add mustard seeds, cumin seeds, urad dal, asafoetida powder, dried red chili and curry leaves. Stir briefly until the mustard seeds splutter.
4 Pour the tempering over the yogurt mix. Serve chilled with Bisi Bele Huli Anna rice.

Memo: Finely chopped coriander and mint leaves will add flavor to the Pachadi.

Pavakka Kichadi

Bitter Gourd Yogurt Salad　ゴーヤーのヨーグルトサラダ

材料　4人分
ゴーヤー　中2本
お好みの油　大さじ1・1/2
ヨーグルト　1・1/2カップ
塩　適量
| 青唐辛子　1本（みじん）
| 生姜　小さじ1（みじん）
A| ココナッツパウダー　大さじ2
| マスタードシード　小さじ1/4

テンパリング
お好みの油　小さじ1
マスタードシード　小さじ1/2
鷹の爪　1本（半分に切る）
カレーリーフ　4〜6枚

1 ゴーヤーを縦半分に切り薄切りにする。鍋に油を入れ、中火で4〜5分炒める。穴あきおたまでキッチンペーパーの上に取り出し、油を切る。
2 ボウルにヨーグルトを入れ、Aを加えて混ぜ、1と塩を入れてよく混ぜる。
3 テンパリングをする。フライパンに油を入れ、マスタードシードを加えパチパチはじけたら、鷹の爪とカレーリーフを加え香りが立つまでかき混ぜながら炒める。
4 2に3を注ぎ、かき混ぜる。レモンライスやココナッツライスなど、ご飯と一緒に食べる。

バリエーション：ゴーヤーは、油で揚げるとクリスピーになり美味しく召し上がれます。

Vendakai Tayir Pachadi
Fried Okra with Yogurt　オクラのヨーグルトサラダ

材料　4人分
オクラ　150g（3mm幅）
揚げ油　適量

A
| コリアンダーパウダー　小さじ1/4
| チリパウダー　小さじ1/4
| 塩　適量

B
| ヨーグルト　1・1/2カップ
| 生姜　小さじ1（みじん）
| 青唐辛子　1本（みじん）
| ココナッツパウダー　大さじ1

テンパリング
ココナッツオイル　小さじ1
マスタードシード　小さじ1/2
鷹の爪　1本（半分に切る）
カレーリーフ　4〜5枚

1 オクラを素揚げする。鍋に揚げ油を用意し、切ったオクラを揚げる。鮮やかな緑色になったらキッチンペーパーの上にすくい油を切る。
2 Aを混ぜ、揚げたオクラの上にふりかける。
3 Bを深めのボウルに入れ、2を入れて混ぜる。
4 テンパリングをする。フライパンにココナッツオイルを入れ加熱し、マスタードシードを加えパチパチはじけたら鷹の爪とカレーリーフを加えて香りが立つまでかき混ぜながら炒める。
5 3の上に4を注ぎ、冷やして食べる。

バリエーション：オクラは、揚げずに大さじ1の油で4〜5分炒めて調理してもOK。
コリアンダーパウダーやチリパウダーをオプションで追加しても美味しくできます。

Serves 4
150g okra
1/4 teaspoon coriander powder
1/4 teaspoon red chili powder
1・1/2 cups yogurt
1 teaspoon ginger, finely chopped
1 green chili, finely chopped
1 tablespoon grated coconut or dry powdered coconut
salt to taste
oil to deep fry
Tempering
1 teaspoon coconut oil
1/2 teaspoon mustard seeds
1 dried red chili, halved
4-5 curry leaves

1 Top the okra and cut into 3 mm thick slices. Heat the oil in a wok for frying and deep fry the okra until crisp. Drain on kitchen paper.
2 Sprinkle the coriander powder, chili powder and dash of salt over the fried okra and set aside.
3 Place the yogurt in a deep bowl, add the ginger, green chili and coconut. Add the fried okra, salt to taste and mix.
4 Prepare the Tempering. Heat oil in a saucepan. Add mustard seeds and let them splutter. Add dried red chili, curry leaves and stir.
5 Pour the tempering over the yogurt. Serve chilled.

Variation: Instead of deep-frying the okra, saute them in 1 tablespoon of oil for 4-5 minutes, until crisp.
Sprinkle the coriander powder, red chili powder and proceed as above.

Serves 4
2 medium bitter gourd
1・1/2 tablespoon oil
1・1/2 cups yogurt
1green chili, finely chopped
1teaspoon ginger, finely chopped
2 tablespoon coconut, freshly grated
- or powdered coconut
1/4 teaspoon mustard seeds, ground
1/4 teaspoon salt
Tempering
1 teaspoon coconut oil
1/2 teaspoon mustard seeds
1 dried red chili, halved
4-6 curry leaves

1 Cut the bittergourd into thin slices. Heat oil in a saucepan, and saute the bittergourd slices for 4-5 minutes over medium heat, until crisp and golden brown. Remove with a slotted spoon and drain on kitchen paper.
2 Place the yogurt in a bowl. Add chopped green chili, ginger, grated coconut and ground mustard seeds. Add salt to taste, the sautéed bittergourd and mix well.
3 Prepare the Tempering. Heat 1 teaspoon coconut oil in a skillet. Add mustard seeds, dried red chili and curry leaves. Allow the mustard seeds to splutter.
4 Pour the Tempering over the pavakka yogurt mix.
Serve chilled with Lemon Rice, Coconut Rice or plain steamed rice.

Variation: For a crisp version of the Pavakka Kichadi, deep fry the bitter gourd in hot oil, until golden brown. Drain on kitchen paper, and proceed as above.

Thakkali, Vellarikkai, Carrot Kosumalli

Tomato, Cucumber and Carrot Salad
コスマリ（インド風チョップドサラダ）

色とりどりの野菜とレンズ豆のサラダに、マスタードシードとウラド豆を添えた一品。
The crisp vegetables and lentils in this colorful salad are flavored with mustard seeds and urad dal.

材料　4人分
ムング豆（黄）　大さじ1
A
├ トマト　1個（みじん）
├ キュウリ　1本（みじん）
├ 人参　1本（みじん）
├ ココナッツシュレッド　大さじ1
├ 青唐辛子　1本（みじん）
├ コリアンダーリーフ　大さじ1（みじん）
├ レモン汁　大さじ1
└ 塩　適量

テンパリング
お好みの油　小さじ2
マスタードシード　小さじ1
クミンシード　小さじ1
ウラド豆　小さじ1
鷹の爪　1本（半分に切る）
アサファティーダパウダー　1つまみ
カレーリーフ　3〜4枚

1 ムング豆を水に1時間浸けて水を切る。
2 ボウルに1とAを入れてよく混ぜる。
3 テンパリングをする。フライパンに油を入れ加熱し、材料を入れる。マスタードシードがパチパチはじけ、豆の色が変わるまでかき混ぜながら炒める。
4 2の上に3を注ぎ、よく混ぜて食べる。

Serves 4
1 tablespoon yellow mung dal
1 tomato, finely chopped
1 cucumber, finely chopped
1 carrot, peeled, finely chopped
1 tablespoon coconut, freshly grated or dried shredded
1 green chili, finely chopped
1 tablespoon coriander, finely chopped
1 tablespoon lemon juice
salt to taste

Tempering
2 teaspoon oil
1 teaspoon mustard seeds
1 teaspoon cumin seeds
1 teaspoon urad dal
1 dried red chili, halved
pinch of asafoetida powder
3-4 curry leaves

1 Soak the yellow moong dal in 1 cup water for about 1 hour. Drain and set aside.
2 In a mixing bowl, place the tomato, cucumber and carrot. Add the drained moong dal, grated coconut, green chili and coriander leaves. Add salt to taste, lemon juice and mix well.
3 Prepare the Tempering. Heat 2 teaspoon oil in a saucepan. Add mustard seeds, cumin seeds, urad dal, dried red chili, asafoetida powder and curry leaves. Stir briefly until the mustard seeds splutter and the dal changes color.
4 Pour the tempering over the vegetables and mix thoroughly. Serve as aside dish with any meal.

Vellarikkai Kosumalli

Cucumber And Lentil Salad

キュウリコスマリ（インド風キュウリのサラダ)

シャキシャキとした食感のキュウリサラダは、どんなお食事にも合う万能なサイドメニュー。
Fresh, cool and crunchy, this cucumber salad with yellow lentils is a refreshing addition to any meal.

材料　4人分
ムング豆（黄）　大さじ2

A
- キュウリ　2本（みじん）
- ココナッツシュレッド　大さじ3
- コリアンダーリーフ　大さじ1（みじん）
- 青唐辛子　1本（みじん）
- レモン汁　大さじ1
- 塩　適量

テンパリング
お好みの油　小さじ2
マスタードシード　小さじ1
クミンシード　小さじ1
ウラド豆　小さじ1
鷹の爪　1本（半分に切る）
アサファティーダパウダー　1つまみ
カレーリーフ　3～4枚

1 ムング豆を水に1時間浸けて水を切る。
2 ボウルに1とAを入れてよく混ぜる。
3 テンパリングをする。フライパンに油を入れ加熱し、材料を入れる。パチパチはじけ、豆の色が変わるまでかき混ぜながら炒める。
4 2の上に3を注ぎ、よく混ぜて食べる。

Serves 4
2 tablespoon yellow moong dal
2 cucumber, finely chopped
3 tablespoon coconut, freshly grated or dried shredded
1 tablespoon fresh coriander, finely chopped
1 green chili, finely chopped
1 tablespoon lemon juice
salt to taste

Tempering
2 teaspoon oil
1 teaspoon mustard seeds
1 teaspoon cumin seeds
1 teaspoon urad dal
1 dried red chili, halved
pinch of asafoetida powder
3-4 curry leaves

1 Soak the yellow moong dal in 1 cup water for about an hour. Drain and set aside.
2 Place the cucumber in a bowl. Add grated coconut, green chili, drained moong dal, and coriander leaves. Add salt to taste, lemon juice and mix well.
3 Prepare the Tempering. Heat 2 teaspoon oil in a saucepan. Add mustard seeds, cumin seeds, urad dal, dried red chili, asafoetida powder and curry leaves. Stir briefly until the mustard seeds splutter and the dal changes color.
4 Pour the tempering over the cucumber salad and mix thoroughly. Serve as a side dish with rice and sambar.

Vegetable Salad

Indian Spice Box
インドのスパイスボックス

毎日の料理に最も使用されるスパイスは、使いやすいようスパイスボックスに入れられます。一般的なボックスには7つの小さな器があります。スパイス使いに慣れてきたら、お好みのスパイスを詰めてみましょう。

An Indian spice box has seven small containers. Generally, the spices most commonly used in daily cooking are placed in the spice box, for ease of use. For South Indian cooking, the following spices and lentils are included.

The South Indian Thali
南インドのタリー

インドでは、複数の料理を1つのプレートに盛り付ける「タリー」があります。バナナリーフの上に料理を盛る伝統の方式が、現代ではタリーとなって浸透しています。タリーは様々な料理で構成されていますが、定番の料理は以下の通りです。

Traditionally served on a banana leaf, the modern South Indian Thali is made up of a selection of various dishes. Rice is served with an array of side dishes, which usually include the following.

1 **ライス**
白米が定番ですが、違う種類の米が盛られることも。一緒にギーの塊が添えられます。

2 **サンバル**
野菜やレンズ豆から作られるスープ。南インド伝統のコース料理のはじまりの一品。

3 **ラッサム**
辛くてさっぱりしたスープ。南インド料理の第2のコース料理です。

4 **ヨーグルト**
米と一緒に食べるサラダにも使用されるヨーグルト。南インド料理では、米料理のお供です。

5 **ポリヤル**
テンパリングやココナッツで仕上げた野菜や豆の炒め物。

6 **カレー**
米料理にもパンにも合うカレー。中でも野菜カレーが定番です。

7 **コスマリ**
マスタードシードのテンパリングをしたフレッシュな野菜サラダ。

8 **スナック（ワダ・バッジ・ボンダ）**
豆やじゃがいもを成型して焼いたスナックは、チャツネやスープにつけて食べられます。

9 **ピクルス**
様々なピクルスがありますが、自家製のマンゴーピクルスが伝統的。

10 **パパド**
薄焼き煎餅のような、パリパリ食感のパパドは、軽く食べやすいかたちです。

11 **スイーツ**
食事の最後ともなるスイーツ。濃厚な味わいが食事のバランスをとります。

1 **Rice**
A staple dish. Steamed white rice is the best, but you can cook any kind of rice. Hot steaming rice is served with a dollop of ghee.

2 **Sambar**
A soup like curry made of vegetables and lentils. Served with rice, sambar is the traditional first course of a South Indian meal

3 **Rasam**
A thin spicy and tangy soup. Rasam served with rice is the second course of a South Indian meal.

4 **Yogurt**
Plain yogurt is a 'must' in South Indian meal and 'yogurt-rice' is the traditional third course. Yogurt Pachadis is a favorite addition.

5 **Poriyal**
A dry vegetable curry, topped with coconut. You can have one or more of these curries with a meal.

6 **Curry/Kootu**
A wet vegetable curry with a gravy. One or more of these can be included in a meal.

7 **Kosumalli**
A vibrant, crunchy vegetable salad with a tempering of mustard seeds.

8 **Fried Vada**
A fried lentil vada or bonda.

9 **Pickles**
Traditionally home- made mango pickle is the favorite. There are many varieties of pickles available.

10 **Fried papaddums**
Add a crunch that is invaluable to the meal.

11 **Sweet**
A sweet is served as a part of meal. Paal Payasam is the usual favorite.

Snack and Chutney

スナック＆チャツネ

南インドでは、軽食として、またおやつの時間に"スナック"と呼ばれる揚げ物が親しまれています。特に豆で作った生地を揚げるワダは、南インドの至る所に露店が出ていたり、衣をスパイシーに仕上げて調理する"天ぷら"のようなバッジやパコラは、軽食だけでなく、食事のときにも一緒にふるまわれます。どれも野菜や豆の旨みをギュッと閉じ込めて美味しい一品です。お好みのチャツネと一緒に、南インドのスナックを楽しんでみてください。

Paruppu Vada
Chana Dal Vada
プルップワダ（チャナ豆のスナック）

南インドで人気のたんぱく質が豊富な豆のスナック。露店で販売されている定番の一品。
A popular protein-rich, crunchy, South Indian street food.

材料　各12〜15個

チャナ豆　1・1/2カップ
鷹の爪　2本
塩　適量
揚げ油　適量

A
| 玉ねぎ　1個分（みじん）
| 生姜　小さじ1（みじん）
| 青唐辛子　2本（みじん）
| コリアンダーの葉　大さじ2
| カレーリーフ　8〜10枚（ちぎる）

1 豆を洗い、たっぷりの水に2〜3時間浸水させ水を切る。
2 1から大さじ1の豆を取り除いたものを、ブレンダーに入れ、少量の水と鷹の爪を加え、ペースト状に撹拌する。
3 ボウルに2の豆とペースト、A、塩を入れ、手でよく混ぜる。12〜15等分に分け、小判型に成形する。
4 200℃の揚げ油に2〜3個ずつ入れ、ひっくり返しながらきつね色になるまで揚げたらキッチンペーパーの上にすくい油を切る。トマトチャツネとココナッツチャツネを合わせて食べる。

Makes 12-15

1 · 1/2 cup chana dal
2 dried red chilies
1 onion, finely chopped
1 teaspoon ginger, finely chopped
2 green chilies, finely chopped
8-10 curry leaves, chopped
2 table spoon fresh coriander, finely chopped
salt to taste
oil for deep frying

1 Wash and soak the chana dal in 3 cups water, for 2-3 hours. Drain completely. Keep 1 tablespoon of dal aside and transfer the rest of the dal to an electric mixer. Add the dried red chilies and grind to a coarse paste, using minimal water.
2 Transfer the dal mixture to a deep bowl. Add the 1 tablespoon soaked dal that was set aside, chopped onion, ginger, green chili, fresh coriander and curry leaves.
3 Add salt to taste and mix thoroughly. Divide the mixture into 12-15 portions. Flatten to make a smooth disc.
4 Heat oil in a fryer to 200℃, and deep fry the Vada, few at a time, until crisp and golden brown. Drain on kitchen paper and serve hot with Tomato Chutney or Coconut Chutney.

Masala Dal Vada
Mixed Lentil Fritters
マサラワダ（ミックス豆の揚げ物）

ココナッツチャツネと一緒にサーブされる、3種類の豆を使ったティータイムスナック。
This spicy fritter served with coconut chutney, is a favorite tea time snack of the region.

材料　12〜15個

チャナ豆　1カップ
ウラド豆　大さじ2
トゥール豆　大さじ2
塩　適量
揚げ油　適量

A
| 生姜　小さじ1（みじん）
| 青唐辛子　2本（みじん）
| 玉ねぎ　1個分（みじん）
| コリアンダーリーフ　大さじ2（みじん）
| カレーリーフ　8〜10枚（ちぎる）
| アサファティーダパウダー　1つまみ

1 豆を洗い、たっぷりの水に2〜3時間浸水させ水を切る。
2 1と少量の水をブレンダーに入れ、ペースト状に撹拌しボウルに移す。
3 ボウルにAと塩を入れ、手でよく混ぜ合わせる。12〜15等分に分け、小判型に成形する。
4 200℃の揚げ油に2〜3個ずつ入れ、ひっくり返しながらきつね色になるまで揚げたらキッチンペーパーの上にすくい油を切る。オニオンチャツネとコリアンダーチャツネをつけて食べる。

Makes 12-15

1 cup chana dal
2 tablespoon urad dal
2 tablespoon toor dal
1 onion, finely chopped
1 teaspoon ginger, finely chopped
2 green chilies, finely chopped
2 tablespoon fresh coriander, finely chopped
8-10 curry leaves, chopped
pinch of asafoetida powder
salt to taste
oil for deep frying

1 Wash and soak the chana dal, urad dal and toor dal together, in 3 cups water, for 2-3 hours. Drain the water completely and keep aside.
2 Place the dal in an electric mixer, and grind to a coarse paste, using minimal water, as needed.
3 Transfer to a mixing bowl. Add chopped onion, ginger, green chili, curry leaves, chopped coriander and asafoetida powder. Add salt to taste and mix well. Divide into 12-15 portions. Flatten to make a smooth disc.
4 Heat oil in a fryer to 200℃ and deep fry the Vada, few at a time, until crisp and golden brown. Drain on kitchen paper and serve hot with Onion Chutney or Coriander Chutney.

Keerai Vada
Medu Vada

Medu Vada

Savory White Lentil Doughnuts メドワダ（白レンズ豆のドーナッツ）

クリスプ食感で人気のティースナック。温かいサンバルスープとチャツネと合わせて。
This uniquely South Indian crisp-yet-spongy Vada is a popular tea time snack, served with piping hot sambar and chutney.

材料　12〜15個

ウラド豆　1カップ
長粒米　大さじ1
揚げ油　適量
A｜青唐辛子　3〜4本（みじん）
　｜生姜　大さじ1（みじん）
　｜カレーリーフ　6〜8枚（ちぎる）
　｜アサファティーダパウダー　1つまみ
　｜塩　適量

1 ウラド豆と長粒米を洗い、2〜3時間浸水させ水をよく切る。
2 1と少量の水をブレンダーに入れて、ペースト状にする。生地があまり水っぽくならないように気をつける。
3 揚げ油を用意しておく。2をボウルに移し、Aを加えて空気を入れるように手でふんわりとよく混ぜる。
4 手を濡らし、3の生地大さじ1を手にとり、軽く押さえ、水で濡らした人差し指で生地に丸い穴を開けて、200℃の油できつね色になるまで揚げる。キッチンペーパーの上にすくい油を切り、ココナッツチャツネとサンバルと食べる。

メモ：ドーナッツ型ではなく、スプーンですくい落として揚げたり、小判型にしてもOK。
バリエーション：ラッサムやサンバルにワダを浸せば、また違った味わいが楽しめます。

Makes 12-15

1 cup urad dal
1 tablespoon rice
3-4 green chilies, finely chopped
1 tablespoon ginger, finely chopped
pinch of asafoetida powder
6-8 curry leaves, chopped
salt to taste
oil to deep fry

1 Wash and soak the urad dal and rice together, in 2 cups water for 2-3 hours. Drain completely and set aside.
2 Place the drained dal and rice in an electric mixer and blend to a smooth paste, using minimal water. The batter should not be too watery.
3 Transfer the batter to a mixing bowl. Add green chilies, chopped ginger, asafoetida powder, curry leaves and salt to taste. Mix thoroughly with the hand and set aside.
4 Heat the oil in a wok to 200°C for deep-frying. To give a doughnut shape, take a tablespoon of the batter and place it on a wet palm. Flatten the batter slightly and make a hole in the center.
5 Slide the doughnut shaped Vada into the hot oil and deep fry, a few at a time. When one side is done, turn with a slotted spoon. When both sides are golden brown, drain on kitchen paper. Continue the process with the remaining batter. Serve hot with Coconut Chutney and Sambar.

Memo : For a simpler option, take a spoonful of the batter and deep fry as a small ball.
Variation : Vadas soaked in Rasam or Sambar make a juicy appetizer, and are called Rasam Vada and Sambar Vada respectively.

Keerai Vada

Savory Spinach Doughnuts キーライワダ（ほうれん草のドーナッツ）

ほうれん草とレンズ豆で作られる軽い食感のワダ。お気に入りの一品です。
Made with spinach and lentils, the crisp and light Keerai Vada is a favorite tea time snack.

材料　12〜15個

ウラド豆　1カップ
鷹の爪　2本
フェンネルシード　小さじ1/2（つぶす）
揚げ油　適量

A
　ほうれん草　1カップ（みじん）
　玉ねぎ　1個分（みじん）
　青唐辛子　2本
　カレーリーフ　8〜10枚（ちぎる）
　アサファティーダパウダー　1つまみ
　塩　適量

1 豆を洗いたっぷりの水に2〜3時間浸して水気を切る。
2 1に鷹の爪と潰したフェンネルシードを加えてミキサーでペースト状になるまで混ぜる。生地が水っぽくならないように気をつける。
3 揚げ油を用意しておく。その間に、2をボウルに移しAを加え手で空気を入れるようにふんわりとよく混ぜる。
4 手を濡らし、3の生地を大さじ1手にとり、軽く押さえ、水で濡らした人差し指で生地に丸い穴を開けて、200℃の油できつね色になるまで揚げる。キッチンペーパーの上にすくい油を切り、お好みのチャツネをつけて食べる。

メモ：ドーナッツ型ではなく、スプーンですくい落として揚げたり、小判型にしてもOK。
バリエーション：ほうれん草の代わりに細切りしたキャベツを1カップ入れると、キャベツワダができます。

Makes 12-15

1 cup urad dal (white lentil)
2 dried red chilies
1/2 teaspoon fennel seeds, coarsely ground
1 cup spinach, finely chopped
2 green chilies, finely chopped
1 onion, finely chopped
pinch of asafoetida powder
8-10 curry leaves, torn
salt to taste
oil for deep frying

1 Wash and soak the urad dal in 2 cups water for 2-3 hours. Drain the water completely and set aside.
2 Place the drained urad dal in an electric blender. Add dried red chilies, fennel seeds and blend to a coarse paste, adding minimal water, as needed. The batter should be stiff and not too watery.
3 Transfer to a mixing bowl. Add the chopped spinach, green chili, onion, asafoetida powder, and curry leaves. Add salt to taste and mix thoroughly.
4 Heat the oil in a wok to 200℃ for frying.
Prepare the Vada. To give a doughnut shape, take a tablespoon of the batter and place it on a wet palm. Flatten the batter and make a hole in the center.
5 Slide the doughnut shaped Vada into the hot oil and deep fry, a few at a time. When one side is done, turn with a slotted spoon. When both sides are golden brown, drain the Vada on kitchen paper. Continue the process with the remaining batter. Serve hot with Coconut Chutney and Sambar.

Memo : For a simpler option, take a tablespoon of the batter and deep fry as a small ball.
Variation : For Cabbage Vada. Use 1 cup of finely shredded cabbage, instead of the spinach and proceed as above.

Snack Chutney

— Home Remedy —

角質除去＆美肌効果

For smooth skin

Home Body Scrub　ボディスクラブ

ベサン粉　1/2カップ
ターメリックパウダー　小さじ1/2
牛乳　大さじ2

材料をボウルに入れ、なめらかなペーストに混ぜる。角質が気になる部位に10〜15分塗り、自然乾燥させて水ですすぐ。

1/2 cup besan flour
1 tablespoon fresh cream
1/2 teaspoon turmeric powder
2 tablespoon milk

Place the ingredients together in a bowl and mix to a smooth paste. Apply generously on the face and arms and let it dry naturally (10-15 minutes). Rinse with water.

Urulaikizhangu Bonda

Battered Potato Fritters　ボンダ（じゃがいもの揚げ物）

インドの露店で人気の一品。スパイスが効いた衣でコーティングして調理します。
A popular street food across India. This South Indian version is coated in a spiced chickpea batter and deep fried.

材料　12〜15個
じゃがいも　中4〜5個
塩　適量
ターメリックパウダー　小さじ1/2
コリアンダーリーフ　大さじ1（みじん）
揚げ油　適量
A 玉ねぎ　大1個（みじん）
青唐辛子　2本（みじん）
生姜　小さじ1（みじん）

テンパリング
お好みの油　大さじ2
マスタードシード　小さじ1
ウラド豆　小さじ1
カレーリーフ　2〜3枚（ちぎる）
アサファティーダパウダー　1つまみ

衣
ベサン粉　1・1/2カップ
米粉　大さじ1
チリパウダー　小さじ1/2
ターメリックパウダー　小さじ1/2
塩　適量

1 じゃがいもをやわらかくなるまでゆで、皮をむきマッシュする。
2 テンパリングをする。フライパンに油を入れ加熱し、材料を入れる。マスタードシードがパチパチはじけ豆の色が変わるまで、かき混ぜながら加熱する。
3 Aを入れ、さらに2〜3分炒める。1のじゃがいも、塩、ターメリックパウダー、コリアンダーリーフを入れ、よく混ぜながらさらに2〜3分炒める。火からおろして冷ます。
4 粗熱がとれたら12〜15等分にして丸くする。
5 衣を用意する。材料をボウルに入れてかき混ぜたら、水1/3カップを加えて混ぜる。衣の生地は薄くなりすぎないように気をつける。
6 4を5につけながら200℃の油で揚げる。衣がきつね色になったらキッチンペーパーの上にすくい油を切る。コリアンダーチャツネやココナッツチャツネをつけて食べる。

メモ：米粉を入れると、クリスピーな食感がアップします。

Makes 12-15
4-5 medium potatoes
1 onion, finely chopped
2 green chilies, finely chopped
1 teaspoon ginger, finely chopped
1/2 teaspoon turmeric powder
1 tablespoon fresh coriander, finely chopped
salt to taste
Oil for deep frying

Tempering
2 tablespoon oil
1 teaspoon mustard seeds
1 teaspoon urad dal
pinch of asafoetida powder
4-6 curry leaves, torn

Batter for Bonda
1・1/2 cups besan (gram flour)
1 tablespoon rice flour
1/2 teaspoon chili powder
1/2 teaspoon turmeric powder
salt to taste

1 Place the potatoes in a saucepan, add 4-5 cups water and bring to a boil. Cook for 8-10 minutes on medium heat, until tender. Drain and set aside to cool. Peel the skin and mash the potatoes. Set aside.
2 Tempering: Heat 2 tablespoon oil in a saucepan. Add mustard seeds, urad dal, asafoetida powder and curry leaves. Allow the seeds to splutter and the dal to change color.
3 Add the onion, green chilies and ginger. Saute for 2-3 minutes. Add the mashed potatoes, salt to taste, and chopped coriander leaves. Mix well and cook for 2-3 minutes. Remove from heat and cool.
4 Divide into 12-15 balls, shape into small rounds and set aside.
5 Prepare the Batter. In a mixing bowl, combine the besan with the rice flour. Add red chili powder, turmeric powder, and salt to taste. Add about 1/3 cup water to make a smooth batter of semi-thick consistency. The batter should not be too thin.
6 Heat the oil in a wok to 200°C for frying. Dip each potato fritter in the batter to coat evenly, and deep fry until golden brown. Drain on kitchen paper and serve hot with Coriander Chutney or Coconut Chutney

Memo : The rice flour added to the batter, helps to make the bonda crisp.

Urulaikizhangu Vada

Spiced Potato Fritters　ポテトワダ（じゃがいものスパイシー揚げ）

簡単な調理でできるポテトスナック。ココナッツチャツネを合わせて。

A versatile potato snack that is a quick and easy to make and best served with coconut chutney.

材料　12〜15個

じゃがいも　中4〜5個

揚げ油　適量

A
| ベサン粉　大さじ4
| 米粉　大さじ1
| 生姜　小さじ1（みじん）
| 青唐辛子　2本（みじん）
| コリアンダーリーフ　1/4カップ（みじん）
| アサファティーダパウダー　1つまみ
| ターメリックパウダー　小さじ1/2
| 塩　適量

テンパリング

お好みの油　小さじ2

マスタードシード　小さじ1

カレーリーフ　6〜8枚（ちぎる）

1 じゃがいもをやわらかくなるまで茹で、皮をむきマッシュしボウルに入れる。

2 Aを入れて手でよく混ぜる。

3 テンパリングをする。フライパンに油を入れ加熱し、材料を入れる。マスタードシードがパチパチはじけたら2のボウルに入れてよく混ぜ合わせる。

4 3を12〜15等分して、手で丸める。

5 200℃の油で揚げる。きつね色になったらキッチンペーパーの上にすくい油を切る。コリアンダーチャツネやオニオンチャツネをつけて食べる。

Makes 12–15

4-5 medium potatoes

3-4 tablespoon besan (gram flour)

1 tablespoon rice flour

1/2 teaspoon turmeric powder

1 teaspoon ginger, finely chopped

2 green chilies, finely chopped

1/4 cup coriander leaves, finely chopped

pinch of asafoetida powder

salt to taste

oil for deep frying

Tempering

2 teaspoon oil

1 teaspoon mustard seeds

6-8 curry leaves, torn

1 Place the potatoes in a saucepan, add 4-5 cups water and bring to a boil. Cook for 8-10 minutes on medium heat, until tender. Drain and set aside to cool. Peel the skin and mash the potatoes. Set aside.

2 Place the mashed potatoes in a bowl. Add the besan, rice flour, turmeric powder, chopped ginger, green chilies, coriander leaves and asafoetida powder. Add salt to taste, mix thoroughly and set aside.

3 Prepare the Tempering. Heat 2 teaspoon oil in a saucepan, add mustard seeds, curry leaves, and allow the mustard seeds to splutter. Pour the tempering over the mashed potato mixture.

4 Mix well and divide into 12-15 balls. Shape into smooth rounds.

5 Heat the oil in a wok to 200°C for frying. Deep fry the fritters, few at a time, until golden brown. Drain on kitchen paper and serve hot with Coriander Chutney and Onion Chutney.

Javvarisi Urulaikizhangu Vada

Tapioca Potato Patties

タピオカパティース（じゃがいもとタピオカの揚げ物）

じゃがいもとタピオカを使用したサクッと食感のスナック。スパイシーなコリアンダーチャツネを添えて。
A wholesome snack and crunchy appetizer served with spicy Coriander chutney.

材料　12～15個

じゃがいも　中4個
タピオカ　1/2カップ
揚げ油　適量

A
| ピーナッツ　大さじ2（砕く）
| クミンシード　小さじ1（すりつぶす）
| 青唐辛子　2本（みじん）
| 生姜　小さじ1（みじん）
| コリアンダーリーフ　大さじ1（みじん）
| 塩　適量

1 じゃがいもをやわらかくなるまで茹で、皮をむきマッシュする。タピオカはたっぷりの水に10分浸水させる。その後水切りをして、やわらかくなるまで2～3時間置いておく。

2 じゃがいもとタピオカをボウルに入れ、Aを加えてよく混ぜる。

3 12～15等分に分け、手で丸める。手で軽く押して小判型に成形する。

4 揚げ油を200℃の温度に温め、2～3個ずつ油に入れる。ひっくり返して均一なきつね色になったらキッチンペーパーの上にすくい油を切る。コリアンダーチャツネをつけて食べる。

Snack
Chutney

Makes 12-15

4 medium potatoes
1/2 cup tapioca
2 table spoon peanuts, roasted and coarsely ground
1 teaspoon cumin seeds, coarsely ground
2 green chilies, finely chopped
1 teaspoon ginger, finely chopped
1 tablespoon coriander leaves, chopped
salt to taste
oil for deep frying

1 Place the potatoes in a saucepan, add 4-5 cups water and bring to a boil. Cook for 8-10 minutes on medium heat, until tender. Drain and set aside to cool. Peel the skin and mash the potatoes. Set aside.

2 Soak the tapioca in cold water for 10 minutes. Drain and set aside for 2-3 hours, until the seeds expand and turn soft.

3 Place the mashed potatoes and tapioca in a bowl. Add the coarsely ground peanuts, cumin seeds, green chilies, ginger and fresh coriander. Add salt to taste and mix thoroughly.

4 Divide the mix into 12-15 balls. Press each ball to make a smooth flat disc.

5 Heat the oil in a wok to 200℃ for deep frying. Fry the patties, few at a time to a golden brown. Drain on kitchen paper and serve with Coriander Chutney.

Vegetable Fritters バッジ（野菜のフリッター）

Bhajji

Vengaya Pakora

Onion Fritters オニオンパコラ（玉ねぎの揚げ物）

フラットにした野菜のフリッター。スパイシーに味つけした衣が野菜の美味しさを引き立たせます。
Bhaji is a flat, spicy vegetable fritter. Potato, eggplant, onion and cauliflower Bhajjis are some of my favorites.

材料　4人分
じゃがいも　2個（2mmスライス）
なす　2本（3mmスライス）
カリフラワー　小房8〜12個
揚げ油　適量
衣
ベサン粉　1カップ
米粉　1/4カップ
チリパウダー　小さじ1/2
ターメリックパウダー　小さじ1/2
アサファティーダパウダー　1つまみ
塩　適量

1　切った野菜をバッドの上に用意しておく。
2　衣を準備する。ボウルにベサン粉と米粉を合わせる。残りの材料を加えて混ぜたら水3/4カップを加え、10分置いて生地をなじませる。
3　鍋に200℃の揚げ油を用意する。野菜に均一に衣につけながら揚げる。
4　きつね色になったらキッチンペーパーの上にすくい油を切る。コリアンダーチャツネやタマリンドチャツネと食べる。

Serves 4
2 potatoes, cut into 2 mm slices
2 eggplant, cut into 3 mm slices
8-12 cauliflower florets
Batter
1・1/2 cup besan (gram flour)
1/4 cup rice flour
1/2 teaspoon cumin seeds, coarsely ground
1/2 teaspoon red chili powder
1/2 teaspoon turmeric powder
pinch of asafoetida powder
1/2 cup water
salt to taste
oil to deep fry

1　Prepare the vegetables on a plate and set aside.
2　Prepare the batter. In a bowl, combine the besan with rice flour. Add ground cumin seeds, coriander powder, red chili powder, turmeric powder, asafoetida powder and salt to taste. Add the water gradually to make a batter of pouring consistency. (Batter should not be too thin)
3　Heat oil in a wok to 200℃ for deep frying. Dip the vegetables in the batter and turn to coat evenly.
4　Deep fry the vegetables, few at a time, until crisp and golden brown. Remove with a slotted spoon and drain on kitchen paper. Serve hot with Coriander chutney or Tamarind chutney.

玉ねぎの甘みが引き立つ一品。お茶と一緒に、またおかずとしても。
Crunchy and delicious when served piping hot, Onion Fritters are generally served as a tea time snack.

材料　15〜18個
ターメリックパウダー　小さじ1/2
チリパウダー　小さじ1/2
塩　適量
揚げ油　適量
A｜ベサン粉　1カップ
　｜米粉　1/4カップ
B｜玉ねぎ　2個（スライス）
　｜生姜　小さじ1（おろし）
　｜青唐辛子　2本（みじん）
　｜コリアンダーリーフ　大さじ2（みじん）

1　ボウルにAを入れ混ぜる。
2　続いてBを加えてよく混ぜ、ターメリックパウダー、チリパウダー、塩を入れて混ぜる。
3　そこに水を1/3カップ徐々に加え、混ぜ合わせる。生地が水っぽくならないようにする。
4　鍋に200℃の揚げ油を用意する。3をスプーンですくい、軽く手で押さえてから熱い油に落とす。きつね色になりカリッとするまで揚げる。溝の開いたスプーンで取り出し、キッチンペーパーの上にすくい油を切る。
5　熱いうちにコリアンダーチャツネやタマリンドチャツネと食べる。

Makes 15-18
1 cup besan (gram flour)
1/4 cup rice flour
2 onions, sliced thin
1 teaspoon ginger, grated
2 green chilies, finely chopped
2 tablespoon fresh coriander, finely chopped
1/2 teaspoon red chili powder
1/2 teaspoon turmeric powder
1/3 cup water
salt to taste
oil to deep fry

1　In a bowl, combine the besan with the rice flour and mix.
2　Add the sliced onion, ginger, green chilies, coriander leaves, turmeric powder and red chili powder. Add salt to taste and mix with the hand.
3　Add water gradually to make a coarse mix. The mix should be dry and not too watery.
4　Heat the oil in a wok to 200℃ for frying. Take spoonful of the onion mix, flatten it slightly and slide into the hot oil. Deep fry until crisp and golden brown. Drain with a slotted spoon and place on kitchen paper.
5　Serve hot with Coriander chutney or Tamarind chutney.

Chutney

チャツネ

Vengaya Chutney
Onion Chutney オニオンチャツネ

玉ねぎとタマリンドの旨みが特徴のチャツネ。パンやスナックと合わせるとバランスよい風味になります。

Sweet onion and tart tamarind create a perfect balance of flavors to serve with snacks and breads.

材料　1カップ分
- | ウラド豆　小さじ1
- A チャナ豆　小さじ1
- | 鷹の爪　2本
- お好みの油　大さじ1
- 玉ねぎ　中2個（スライス）
- 塩　適量
- タマリンドペースト　小さじ1/2

テンパリング
- お好みの油　小さじ1
- 鷹の爪　1本（半分に切る）
- カレーリーフ　4〜5枚

1 フライパンに油大さじ1を入れ加熱する。Aを入れ、豆の色が変わるまでかき混ぜながら炒める。
2 そこに玉ねぎを入れ、塩をふりきつね色になるまで5〜7分炒める。タマリンドペーストを加えて混ぜ、火からおろして粗熱をとる。
3 ブレンダーに2移して、粒が残る程度に撹拌したら塩で味をととのえる。
4 テンパリングをする。フライパンに油を入れ加熱し、材料を入れ、マスタードシードがパチパチはじけたら火をとめ、チャツネの上にかける。

バリエーション：玉ねぎと一緒に、にんにく2〜3片（みじん）を炒めて加えると、香り豊かになります。

Makes 1 cup
- 1 tablespoon oil
- 1 teaspoon urad dal
- 1 teaspoon chana dal
- 2 dried red chilies
- 2 medium onions, coarsely chopped
- 1/2 teaspoon tamarind paste
- salt to taste

Tempering
- 1 teaspoon oil
- 1/2 teaspoon mustard seeds
- 1 dried red chili, halved
- 4-5 curry leaves

1 Heat 1 tablespoon oil in a saucepan. Add urad dal, chana dal and dried red chilies. Stir briefly until the dals turn golden.
2 Add the onions and salt to taste. Saute for 5-7 minutes until the onions are nicely browned. Add the tamarind paste and mix. Remove from heat and cool.
3 Place the sauteed onion mix in an electric blender and grind to a smooth paste. Transfer to a serving dish.
4 Tempering for Chutney. Heat 1 teaspoon oil in a saucepan, add mustard seeds, dried red chili and curry leaves. When the mustard seeds splutter, remove from heat and pour over the Onion Chutney. Serve with Dosa, Paniyaram or Vada.

Variation：Add 2-3 cloves of garlic to the onions and saute until well browned. Procced as above.

Puli Chutney
Tamarind Chutney タマリンドチャツネ

エキゾチックな甘酸っぱい風味で、バッジやパコラなどの軽食の風味を豊かにします。

This exotic sweet and sour chutney is a delicious condiment which compliments snacks such as Bhajji and Pakora.

材料　1カップ分
- タマリンドペースト　大さじ2
- 黒糖　3/4カップ
- 岩塩　小さじ3/4
- 塩　小さじ1/4
- チリパウダー　小さじ1/2
- クミンシード　小さじ1/2（ロースト）
- ジンジャーパウダー　小さじ1/2

1 タマリンドペーストを水1カップに溶かしておく。
2 ブレンダーでペースト状に撹拌し、さらにその他の材料をすべてブレンダーに入れペースト状にする。黒糖が溶けるまで撹拌する。
3 黒糖と塩で味をととのえる。必要な場合、水を加えてお好みのやわらかさにする。バッジ、ボンダなどと合わせて食べる。

メモ：冷凍庫で2ヵ月保存可能です。

Kothamalli Chutney

Coriander Chutney コリアンダーチャツネ

フレッシュなコリアンダーの風味が活きたチャツネは、スナックなどの軽食やパンと合わせても。

A spicy dip of fresh coriander, ginger, coconut and chilies to serve with snacks like Tapioca Patties and Upma.

材料　1カップ分

コリアンダーリーフ　3カップ
青唐辛子　3〜4本
生姜　2〜3枚（スライス）
クミンシード　小さじ1/2（ロースト）
ココナッツパウダー　大さじ2
黒糖　小さじ1/4
レモン汁　大さじ1
塩　適量

1 コリアンダーリーフをよく洗い、水を切る。茎の部分を含め、やわらかいところすべて使用する。
2 ブレンダーにコリアンダーリーフとその他のすべての材料と少量の水を入れ、ペースト状に撹拌する。
3 器に盛り、ボンダやバッジ、パコラなどと合わせて食べる。

メモ：フレッシュなコリアンダーを使用することで、美味しいチャツネができあがります。作ったら密閉容器に入れて冷蔵庫で保存し、1週間以内に食べましょう。

バリエーション：ローストひよこ豆またはピーナッツを大さじ1加えると、濃厚な味わいに仕上がります。

Makes 1 cup

3 cups fresh coriander
3-4 green chilies
2 small slices of ginger
1/2 teaspoon cumin seeds, roasted
2 tablespoon freshly grated coconut or powdered coconut
1/4 teaspoon jaggery
salt to taste
1 tablespoon lemon juice

1 Wash, drain and chop the coriander leaves with its tender stems.
2 Place the chopped coriander in an electric blender. Add green chilies, cumin seeds, ginger, coconut, jaggery. Add salt to taste, and lemon juice. Blend to a smooth paste, using 1-2 tablespoon of water.
3 Transfer to a bowl and serve with Bonda, Vegetable Bhajji and Pakora.

Memo：Coriander chutney tastes best when freshly prepared. Keep in an air-tight container and place in the refrigerator for use over a couple of days.

Variation：For a thicker chutney, add 1 tablespoon of ground dalia(roasted gram) or peanuts to the ingredients and proceed as above.

Makes 1 cup

2 tablespoon tamarind paste
3/4 cup jaggery
3/4 teaspoon rock salt
1/4 teaspoon salt
1/2 teaspoon red chili powder
1/2 teaspoon cumin seeds, roasted, coarsely ground
1/2 teaspoon ground ginger powder

1 Dissolve the tamarind paste in 1 cup water. Transfer to a saucepan.
2 Add the jaggery, rock salt, red chili powder, ground cumin, black pepper, and ginger powder. Bring to a boil, and simmer for 3-4 min until the mixture thickens slightly. Stir the mixture, until the jaggery is well dissolved.
3 Adjust the taste. Add a little more salt and jaggery, if needed. Transfer to a bowl and serve with Pakoras, Bhajji and Bonda.

Memo：Tamarind chutney can be kept in the freezer for up to two months.

Thakkali Chutney

Tomato Chutney トマトチャツネ

サルサのようなこのチャツネは、ワダやティフィンと相性抜群。

This colorful and tart, salsa-like chutney is another delightful accompaniment to tiffin items such as Paruppu Vada.

材料　1カップ分
お好みの油　大さじ1
玉ねぎ　1/2個
トマト　3個（角切り、カットトマト缶の場合250g）
塩　適量

A ┌ ウラド豆　小さじ1
　│ フェヌグリーグシード　5～7粒
　│ 鷹の爪　2本
　└ 黒胡椒　4～5粒

テンパリング
お好みの油　小さじ2
鷹の爪　1本（半分に切る）
マスタードシード　小さじ1/2
アサファティーダパウダー　1つまみ
カレーリーフ　4～6枚

1 フライパンに油を入れ中火で加熱する。Aを入れ、豆の色が変わるまで炒める。
2 お好みで玉ねぎを加え、2～3分炒める。トマトを加え、塩で味をととのえる。トマトがやわらかくなるまでフタをして3～5分加熱する。
3 ブレンダーに移し、なめらかなペースト状にして器に盛る。
4 テンパリングをする。フライパンに油を入れ加熱する。材料を入れ、マスタードシードがパチパチとはじけるまでかき混ぜる。
5 4を3の上に注ぎ、よく混ぜる。

メモ：玉ねぎを加えることにより、チャツネに自然な甘さが加わります。
バリエーション：にんにく2片、クローブ2粒をAに加えるとガーリックトマトチャツネができます。
ピーナッツ大さじ1をAに加えるとトマトピーナッツチャツネができます。ピーナッツを入れることにより、濃厚でナッツ風味の広がるチャツネに仕上がります。

Makes 1 cup
1 tablespoon oil
1 tea spoon urad dal
5-7 fenugreek seeds
2 dried red chilies
4-5 black peppercorns
3 tomatoes, chopped or 250g canned tomato
1/2 onion
salt to taste

Tempering for Chutney
2 teaspoon oil
1/2 teaspoon mustard seeds
1 dried red chili, halved
pinch of asafoetida powder
4-6 curry leaves

1 Heat 1 tablespoon oil in a saucepan, over medium heat. Add urad dal, fenugreek seeds, black peppercorns, red chili and stir briefly, until the dal changes color.
2 Add the onions and saute for 2-3 minutes. Add chopped tomatoes, and salt to taste. Cook covered for 3-5 minutes, until the tomatoes soften. Remove from heat and cool.
3 Place the mixture in an electric mixer and blend to a smooth paste. Transfer to a serving bowl.
4 Prepare the Tempering. Heat 2 teaspoon of oil in a small saucepan. Add mustard seeds, dried red chili, asafoetida powder, curry leaves and allow the mustard seeds to splutter.
5 Pour over the tomato chutney and mix well. Serve with snacks such as Bonda and Masala Dal Vada,

Memo: Peanuts lend a nuttier flavor and a thicker consistency to the chutney.
The onion adds a natural sweetness and volume to the chutney.
Variation: For Garlic Tomato Chutney. Add 2 cloves of garlic and saute with urad dal and rest of the ingredients. Proceed as above.
For Tomato Peanut Chutney: Add 1 tablespoon of peanuts to the urad dal, and stir briefly. Grind together with the rest of the ingredients.

Thengai Chutney

Coconut Chutney ココナッツチャツネ

南インドで最もポピュラーなチャツネ。ほぼすべてのスナックやティフィンに添えられます。

Among the most versatile chutneys , this creamy coconut condiment is served with almost every snack and tiffin dish.

材料　1カップ分

A
| ココナッツパウダー　3/4カップ
| 青唐辛子　2本
| 生姜　2枚（スライス）
| 塩　適量

テンパリング

お好みの油　小さじ2
マスタードシード　小さじ1/2
鷹の爪　1本（半分に切る）
アサファティーダパウダー　1つまみ
カレーリーフ　4〜6枚

1 Aをブレンダーに加え撹拌する。なめらかなペースト状になったらボウルに移す。
2 テンパリングをする。フライパンに油を入れて中火にかけ、マスタードシードを入れる。パチパチとはじけてきたら、残りの材料を加える。豆の色が変わるまで炒める。
3 1の上に2を注ぎ、よく混ぜる。ドーサ、イドリ、ワダなどと食べる。密閉容器に入れて冷蔵庫で保存する。

メモ：ローストひよこ豆を加えることにより、厚みのあるチャツネになります。ひよこ豆がない場合はローストピーナッツまたはチャナ豆で代用してもOK。
バリエーション：タマリンドパルプ小さじ1/4、玉ねぎ1/4個（みじん）をAに加えるとタマリンドココナッツチャツネができます。
コリアンダーリーフ1/2カップ、玉ねぎ1/4個（みじん）、ヨーグルト大さじ2またはレモン汁 小さじ2をAに加えるとグリーンココナッツチャツネができます。

Makes 1 cup

3/4 cup fresh coconut, grated or powdered coconut
2 green chilies
2 small slices ginger
salt to taste

Tempering

2 teaspoon oil
1/2 teaspoon mustard seeds
1 dried red chili, halved
pinch of asafoetida powder
4-6 curry leaves

1 Place the grated coconut in a blender. Add green, chilies and ginger. Add about 1/4 cup of water, salt to taste and grind to a smooth paste. Transfer to a bowl.
2 Tempering for Chutney. Heat oil in a small saucepan, over medium heat. Add mustard seeds, and allow them to splutter. Add dried red chili, asafoetida powder, and curry leaves.
3 Pour the tempering over the Coconut Chutney and mix well. Serve with Dosa, Idli and Vada. Place in an air-tight container and store in the refrigerator.

Memo：1 tablespoon roasted gram adds volume to the chutney. Peanuts are a good substitute for roasted gram.
Variation：For Tamarind Coconut Chutney. Add 1/4 teaspoon tamarind paste, 1/4 onion to rest of the ingredients and blend to a smooth paste. Add the tempering as above.
For Green Coconut Chutney: Add 1/2 cup fresh coriander and 2 teaspoon lemon juice to the above ingredients and blend to a smooth paste. Add the tempering as above.

Snack
Chutney

Tiffin

ティフィン（一品料理）

米や豆、セモリナ小麦をベースに作られる食事を、南インドでは「ティフィン」と呼び、一品料理として楽しんでいます。ドーサやウッタパン、ペサラットゥは南インド独自の料理で、原料が米と豆からできている生地で作られるため、カレーやスープ、サラダと一緒にサーブして楽しめる料理です。米と豆の基本の生地は発酵が必要ですが、オーブンの予熱などを利用すれば簡単にできます。ヘルシーかつ南インドならではやみつきになる味わいを楽しんでください。

基本の生地
Batter for Dosa and Idli

南インドの中で最も人気のある料理が、米と豆の生地を焼いたドーサとイドリ。
ご家庭でも簡単にできるドーサとイドリの基本の生地をご紹介します。

Dosa and Idli are the most popular South Indian breakfast dishes, and arguably the most delicious. Here is the basic proportion widely used to make Idli and Dosa batter at home.

長粒米　3カップ
ウラド豆　1カップ
塩　適量

1　長粒米とウラド豆は、それぞれ洗いたっぷりの水に4〜5時間浸水させ、水を切る。
2　ブレンダーに長粒米と水1カップを入れて、粒がわずかに残るくらいに撹拌し、大きめのボウルに移す。
3　ブレンダーにウラド豆を入れて撹拌する。冷水3/4カップを徐々に加えながら4〜5分撹拌し、空気を含ませてなめらかにする。
4　2に3を加え、生地に空気を入れるように、しばらく手でかき混ぜる。
5　4の温度が人肌程度になったら、ボウルにラップをかぶせ、一晩（10〜12時間）置き、発酵させる。生地が2倍近くの量になり、軽く泡立っているのが発酵の目安。
6　盛り付ける器の準備がととのったら、生地に塩を加え、一枚一枚焼く。

メモ：冬場などは、使用した後のオーブンの予熱などを活用して発酵できます。
生地を一度で使い切らない場合は、密閉し数日冷蔵庫で保存OK。
使用する際は、生地のやわらかさをみて、固いようであれば水を加えましょう。
冷凍すれば約1ヵ月保存が可能です。使用するときは、常温解凍して使用しましょう。

バリエーション：フェヌグリーグシード小さじ1をウラド豆と一緒に浸水させ、生地に加えると焼き上がりがふわふわになります。

3 cups parboiled rice, regular rice or long grain rice
1 cup urad dal
salt to taste

1　Wash and soak the rice and urad dal separately in water for 3-4 hours. Drain the water and set aside.
2　Place the drained rice in an electric mixer, and gradually add about 1 cup of water, grinding it to a paste of slightly grainy texture. Transfer the batter to a deep bowl and set aside.
3　Next, place the drained urad dal in an electric mixer. Add about 3/4 cup water gradually, grinding the dal for up to about 4-5 minutes, until it blends to a smooth paste. The batter will feel light and fluffy.
4　Combine the dal batter with the rice batter and mix thoroughly with your hand. The warmth of the hand will initiate the fermentation process. The batter should be in a sufficiently large bowl, since it increases in volume after fermentation.
5　Cover the bowl and set aside to ferment for 10-12 hours, or overnight. The batter will rise and increase to almost double its volume. It will be lighter and will have a fermented smell. Now it is ready to make idli and dosa.
6　Add salt to the batter, when ready to make the dish.

Memo: In the wintertime, to aid the fermentation process, place the batter in a warm pre heated oven. The oven should be turned off before placing the bowl with the batter in it.
Once ready, place the batter in an airtight container and keep in the fridge for up to a week, for later use.
When ready to use, take a portion of the batter, adjust the consistency with a little water and add salt to taste.
The dosa batter can be kept in freezer for up to a month. Bring it to room temperature before use.

Variation: 1 teaspoon of fenugreek seeds, added to the urad dal will aid the fermentation process. The batter will give softer Idli and crispier Dosa. Soak and grind with the urad dal and proceed as above.

Dosa

Rice and Lentil Crepes　ドーサ（米と豆のクレープ）

南インド独自のクレープ料理。長粒米とウラド豆を発酵させた生地で作ります。
Unique to South India, Dosa is a savory crepe made of a fermented batter of rice and urad dal.

材料　15〜20枚分
基本の生地（P99）
塩　少々
ギーもしくはゴマ油　適宜

1 P99にしたがい基本の生地を作り、塩を混ぜる。平たいクレープ用フライパンを準備する。
2 ボウルに生地を入れ、少量の水を入れてよく混ぜる。
3 フライパンを加熱し、薄く油をひき適度な温度にする。少量の水をふりかけ、すぐに蒸発するくらいが目安。
4 丸いおたまで生地をすくい、フライパンの中央に注ぐ。おたまの底で中心から円を描き、直径20〜25cmに広げていく。
5 小さじ1の油を生地の外側にたらし、生地がきつね色に変わるまで1〜2分加熱する。生地の外側が反り返ってきたらフライ返しで裏返し、片面をさらに1分加熱する。
6 焼き上がった生地は、フライパンの上で成型し、器に盛る。次の生地を焼く前には、フライパンに水をふりかけ温度をもとし、弱火にしてキッチンペーパーなどで拭き取ってから行う。ココナッツチャツネやサンバルと食べる。

Dosa Shape　ドーサの形状

ドーサは、焼きたてのうちに様々な形状にして器に盛ります。盛り付け方は、次の3つの形状があります。
Form the dosa into a variety of shapes. Serve while hot.

筒型	円形の端から反対方向に丸めて成型する。器に盛る際は重なる部分を底にする。マサラドーサなど具を詰める際は、先に具を中心に置いてから成型する。	**Rolled Dosa**	The dosa may be folded from both sides to make a roll. If using a stuffing for the dosa, place the filling in the center of the dosa, and fold the two sides. Serve with the folds at the bottom.
半月型	端と端を合わせて成型する。プレーンの場合はもちろん、具を詰める際にも成型される。	**Moon Dosa**	Fold the top edge of the dosa to give a moon shape.
円柱型	まな板などに生地を置き、中心から外側に包丁で切れ目を入れ、重ね合わせて成型する。プレーンの場合に多く成型される。	**Cone Dosa**	Cut in a slit from the center of the dosa towards the outside. Roll to form a cone shape. This shape is common for plain dosa.

Makes 15-20

1 portion dosa batter (P99)

salt to taste

ghee or sesame oil

1 Prepare the Dosa batter as per instructions on P99

2 Place a portion of the dosa batter in a bowl. Add a little water to bring it to a thick pouring consistency.

3 Heat a non-stick tava or flat sausepan. Sprinkle a little water. When the water sizzles, the tava is ready for use. Wipe it with the kitchen roll and reduce the heat.

4 Pour a ladleful of the batter in the center of the tava. Spread quickly, using a spiral motion going outwards until the dosa is about 20-25 cm in diameter. Increase the heat to medium.

5 Pour 1 teaspoon of ghee or sesame oil around the edges. Cook for 1-2 minutes, until the edges start to curl and the base turns golden brown. Flip over and cook the other side for a minute.

6 Fold the Dosa and transfer to a serving plate. Before making the next Dosa, reduce the heat, sprinkle some water on the tava and wipe with a towel to cool it. Pour a ladleful of the batter and repeat the process. Serve hot with Coconut Chutney and Sambar.

Dosa Masala

Potato and Onion Masala ポテトマサラ（じゃがいもと玉ねぎのマサラ）

ピリッと辛く味付けされたじゃがいもと玉ねぎを炒めたポテトマサラは、そのままはもちろん、ドーサの詰め物としても。
This lightly spiced potato and onion mixture, tempered with mustard seeds and curry leaves, is a favorite filling for dosa.

材料　4人分
じゃがいも　4個
玉ねぎ　2個（スライス）
青唐辛子　1本（みじん）
生姜　大さじ1（みじん）
ターメリックパウダー　小さじ1/2
チリパウダー　小さじ1/2
塩　適量
コリアンダーリーフ　適量
テンパリング
お好みの油　大さじ1
マスタードシード　小さじ1/2
クミンシード　小さじ1/2
ウラド豆　小さじ1/2
鷹の爪　2本
アサファティーダパウダー　1つまみ
カレーリーフ　4〜6枚（ちぎる）

1 たっぷりのお湯でじゃがいもをやわらかくゆでる。水を切り、皮をむき粗くマッシュする。
2 テンパリングをする。フライパンに油を入れ加熱し、材料を加える。パチパチはじけ、豆の色が変わるまで、かき混ぜながら炒める。
3 玉ねぎ、青唐辛子、生姜を加え、玉ねぎが半透明になるまで3〜4分炒める。
4 1を加えてよく混ぜ、ターメリックパウダー、チリパウダー、塩を加えてさらに混ぜる。お好みで少量の水を入れてやわらかくする。中火で3〜4分加熱して味をなじませる。お好みでコリアンダーリーフを散らす。あらかじめ作っておいたマサラを焼きたてのドーサに包み、器に盛る。プリなどと一緒に食べる。

Serves 4
4 potatoes, boiled
2 onions, sliced
1 green chili, chopped
1 teaspoon ginger, finely chopped
1/2 teaspoon turmeric powder
1/2 teaspoon red chili powder
salt to taste

Tempering
1 tablespoon oil
1/2 teaspoon mustard seeds
1/2 teaspoon cumin seeds
1/2 teaspoon urad dal
2 dried red chilies
pinch of asafoetida powder
4-6 curry leaves, torn

1 Place the potatoes in a saucepan, add 4-5 cups water and cook for 8-10 minutes, on medium heat until tender. Drain and set aside to cool. Peel the skin and mash coarsely.
2 Prepare the Tempering. Heat 1 tablespoon oil in a saucepan. Add the mustard seeds, cumin seeds, urad dal, dried red chili, asafoetida powder and curry leaves. Stir briefly until the mustard seeds splutter and the dals change color.
3 Add the onions, ginger, green chilies and saute for 3-4 minutes, until the onions are translucent.
4 Add the mashed potatoes and mix. Add turmeric powder, red chili powder and salt to taste. Add 3-4 tablespoon of water and cook covered for 3-4 minutes to allow the flavors to blend. Serve as a filling for Dosa or a side dish with Poori.

Idli

Steamed Rice Cake　イドリ（米蒸しパン）

米と豆からできた一口サイズの蒸しパンです。南インドの家庭では朝食としてふるまわれています。

A breakfast staple in most South Indian homes, Idli is a delicately flavored savory cake.

材料　25〜30個
基本の生地（P99）
塩　適量
お好みの油　適量

1 P99にしたがい基本の生地を準備し塩を加える。
2 イドリの専用の型に薄く油を塗る。
3 型に生地を大さじ1ずつ流し入れたら、水を張った鍋に型を入れる。12〜15分蒸して生地がふわふわになったら取り出し、粗熱をとる。
4 バターナイフ等を使い、型から取り出す。ココナッツチャツネやサンバルと合わせて食べる。

バリエーション：焼き上がったイドリを半分に切り、マスタードシード少量とチリパウダー1つまみをテンパリングした油と炒めるとカリカリの食感を楽しめます。

Makes 25-30
1 portion Idli batter (P99)
salt to taste
oil to grease the Idli mould

1 Prepare the Idli batter as per instructions mentioned on P99. Add salt to taste. Mix well and keep aside.
2 Prepare the Idli steamer. Grease the Idli mould with a little oil.
3 Place a heaped tablespoon of the batter in each of the grooves. Steam the idli for 12-15 minutes, over medium heat until it soft and spongy.
4 Gently slide the idli off the mould, with a butter knife. Serve hot with Coconut Chutney and Sambar.

Variation : Leftover Idli can be cut into half and stir-fried, until crisp with a tempering of oil, mustard seeds and a pinch of chili powder.

The Idli Mould　イドリの型

イドリは、イドリ専用の蒸し器を使用して作ります。蒸し器のくぼみに生地を流し込み、蒸し器ごと水を入れた鍋に入れて加熱します。蒸し上がったら、楊枝などで取り出し、サンバルやココナッツチャツネと一緒に温かいうちに食べます。専用の型がない場合は、小さなボウルやくぼみのある容器に大さじ1の生地を入れて12〜15分蒸します。

An Idli mould and Idori steamer is needed to make Idli. If you do not have an idli mould, use small bowls, or any grooved container. Pour a tablespoon of the idli batter in it and steam for 12-15 minutes, until soft.

Kancheepuram Idli

Savory Rice Cake with Vegetables and Spices

カンチプラムイドリ（野菜とスパイスの米蒸しパン）

イドリに野菜とスパイスを加えたもの。黒胡椒、生姜、チリパウダー、カシューナッツが風味豊かな一品です。
Idli batter is seasoned with whole black pepper, ginger, chilies and cashews.

材料25〜30個分
基本の生地（P99）
インゲン豆　8〜10本（みじん）
人参　1/2本（皮をむきみじん）
生姜　小さじ1（みじん）
青唐辛子　1本（みじん）
黒胡椒　10〜15粒（つぶす）
ターメリックパウダー　1つまみ
アサファティーダパウダー　1つまみ
塩　適量

テンパリング
お好みの油　小さじ2
カシューナッツ　6〜8粒（砕く）
カレーリーフ　6〜8枚

1 P99にしたがい基本の生地をボウルに準備する。
2 インゲン豆、人参を3〜4分ゆで水切りする。
3 1に2とその他の材料を入れて混ぜる。
4 テンパリングをする。フライパンに油、カシューナッツを入れ、きつね色になるまで軽く炒める。さらにカレーリーフを加え炒める。3に加え、よく混ぜ合わせる。
5 イドリの型に薄く油を塗る。
6 型に生地を大さじ1ずつ流し入れたら、水を張った鍋に型を入れる。12〜15分蒸して生地がふわふわになったら取り出し、粗熱をとる。
7 バターナイフなどを使い、型から取り出す。オニオンチャツネやベジタブルサンバルと合わせて食べる。

Makes 25-30
1 portion idli batter (P99)
8-10 green beans, finely cut
1/2 carrot, peeled, finely chopped
1 teaspoon ginger, finely chopped
1 green chili, finely chopped
10-15 black peppercorns, coarsely ground
pinch of turmeric powder
pinch of asafoetida powder
salt to taste

Tempering
2 teaspoon oil
6-8 cashews, broken
6-8 curry leaves, torn

1 Prepare the Idli batter as per instructions mentioned on P99.
2 In a small saucepan, place 1 cup water and bring it to a boil. Add the beans, carrots, and a little salt to it. Cook for 3-4 minutes over medium heat, until the vegetables are tender. Drain and set aside.
3 Place the idli batter in a bowl. Add the cooked beans and carrots. Add ginger, green chilies, ground peppercorns, turmeric powder, asafoetida powder and salt to taste. Mix well and set aside.
4 Prepare the Tempering. Heat the oil in a saucepan. Add the cashews and saute them lightly, until browned. Add curry leaves and stir briefly. Add the tempering to the prepared batter and mix thoroughly.
5 Grease the Idli mould with a little oil and prepare the steamer.
6 Place a heaped tablespoon of the batter in each of the grooves. Steam the idli for 12-15 minutes, until it soft and spongy.
7 Gently slide the Idli off the Idli mould, with a butter knife. Serve hot with Onion Chutney and Vegetable Sambar.

Tiffin

Kuzhi Paniyaram

Spiced Rice Balls パニヤラム（スパイスライスボール）

米と豆の生地から作る、クリスプ食感と味わい豊かなライスボール。青唐辛子の爽やかな辛みが特徴です。
Crisp and flavorful, made from a batter of urad dal and rice, mixed with chopped onions and green chilies.

材料　4人分
基本の生地　1/2量（P99）
玉ねぎ　1個（みじん）
お好みの油　適量
青唐辛子　3本（みじん）
　｜　生姜　大さじ1（みじん）
A　コリアンダーリーフ　大さじ1（みじん）
　｜　塩　適量

テンパリング
お好みの油　小さじ2
マスタードシード　小さじ1
ウラド豆　小さじ2
カレーリーフ　6〜8枚

Serves 4
1/2 portion batter for Idli (P99)
1 onions, finely chopped
3 green chilies, finely chopped
1 teaspoon ginger, grated
1 tablespoon fresh coriander leaves, finely chopped
salt to taste

Tempering
2 teaspoon oil
1 teaspoon mustard seeds
1 teaspoon urad dal
pinch of asafoetida
6-8 curry leaves, torn

1 基本の生地をボウルに用意する。
2 テンパリングをする。フライパンに油を入れ加熱し、材料を加える。パチパチはじけ、豆の色が変わるまでかき混ぜながら炒める。
3 玉ねぎを加えて2〜3分炒め、Aを加えてかき混ぜる。
4 1に3を入れ、よく混ぜる。
5 専用のフライパンを熱し、油をひく。
6 生地を流し込み、中火で3〜4分焼く。楊枝などを使い生地をまわしながら焼く。表面に均等に焼き色がついたら取り出し、ココナッツチャツネやトマトチャツネ、サンバルと一緒に食べる。

メモ：専用のフライパンがない場合は、たこ焼き器で代用できます。

バリエーション：玉ねぎをココナッツパウダー大さじ2に変更すると、ココナッツのフレーバーが楽しめます。

1 Prepare the batter as per instructions on P99. Add salt to taste. Place a portion of the batter in a bowl. Add salt to taste.
2 Prepare the tempering. Heat 2 teaspoon oil in a saucepan. Add mustard seeds, urad dal, asafoetida powder and curry leaves. Allow the mustard seeds to splutter and the dal to change color.
3 Add chopped onions and saute for 2-3 minutes, until lightly browned. Add green chilies and ginger.
4 Pour the tempering over the prepared batter and mix well.
5 Grease a grooved Paniyaram vessel and turn on the heat. Pour a heaped teaspoon of the batter into each depression. Cover and cook for 3-4 minutes, over medium beat. Use a skewer to turn the Paniyaram. Cook both sides until evenly browned.
6 Transfer to a serving bowl, and repeat with rest of the batter. Serve hot with Coconut Chutney or Tomato Chutney and Sambar.

Variation : Add 2 tablespoon of fresh shredded coconut, instead of the onion and proceed as above.

Pesarettu

Split Green Gram Dosa ペサラットゥ（ムング豆のドーサ）

アンドラ州で作られるムング豆をたっぷり使用した一品。スパイシーに味つけした玉ねぎをトッピングしていただきます。
A delicacy from Andhra Pradesh, this protein-rich dosa is topped with spiced onions and served with Tomato Chutney.

材料10〜12枚
ムング豆（緑）　2カップ
長粒米　1/2カップ
アサファティーダパウダー　1つまみ
コリアンダーリーフ　大さじ2（みじん）
塩　適量
お好みの油　適宜

A
┃ 玉ねぎ　1個（みじん）
┃ 鷹の爪　2本
┃ 青唐辛子　2〜3本（みじん）
┃ 生姜　大さじ1（すりおろし）
┃ クミンシード　小さじ1/2（つぶす）

トッピング
お好みの油　大さじ1
玉ねぎ　2個（みじん）
青唐辛子　2本（みじん）
カレーリーフ　6〜8枚
チリパウダー　小さじ1/2
ターメリックパウダー　小さじ1/2

Makes 10-12
2 cups green moong dal
1/2 cup long grain rice
1 onion, chopped finely
2-3 green chilies
1 teaspoon ginger, finely chopped
1/2 teaspoon cumin seeds, coarsely ground
pinch of asafoetida powder
2 tablespoon coriander leaves, finely chopped
salt to taste
oil as required

Onion Topping
1 tablespoon oil
2 medium onions, finely chopped
2 green chilies, finely chopped
1/2 teaspoon chili powder
1/2 teaspoon turmeric powder
6-8 curry leaves

1. ムング米と長粒米は合わせて水洗いし、3カップの水に2〜3時間浸水させる。その後ブレンダーに移す。
2. Aを加え、少量の水を入れてペースト状にする。
3. ボウルに移し、アサファティーダパウダーとコリアンダーリーフ、塩を入れて混ぜる。
4. トッピングをつくる。フライパンに油を入れ加熱し、玉ねぎを強火で2〜3分炒める。
5. 残りの材料と塩を加え、3〜4分加熱し火を止める。
6. 生地を焼く。フライパンを熱し、少量の水を入れ水分を拭き取り、適度な温度にしてから油をひく。
7. 生地をおたまですくい落とし、おたまの底で生地を伸ばしながら直径12〜15cmの円形に広げる。
8. 小さじ1の油を生地の外側にかけまわして火を強め、生地の底に焼き色がつくまで2〜3分加熱する。裏返して反対側も焼き色がつくまで2〜3分加熱する。
9. 器に移し、5をのせて食べる。お好みでココナッツチャツネとトマトチャツネと合わせて食べる。

メモ：生地は発酵の必要がないため簡単に作れますが、発酵させるとより美味しくできあがります。
生地を使い切れない場合は、冷蔵庫で1〜2日保存可能。

1. Wash and soak the green moong dal with the rice in 3 cups water for 2-3 hours. Drain and place in an electric blender.
2. Add onion, green chilies, ginger, cumin seeds, and blend to a coarse paste, using a little water.
3. Transfer the batter to a mixing bowl. Add asafoetida powder, coriander leaves and salt to taste.
4. Prepare the Topping. Heat the oil in a saucepan, and saute the onions over high heat for 2-3 minutes, until slightly charred.
5. Add green chili, turmeric powder, red chili powder, curry leaves and salt to taste. Saute for 3-4 minutes. Remove from heat and keep aside.
6. To make the Pesarettu. Heat the non-stick pan or dosa tava. . Sprinkle a few drops of water over the surface. If the water sizzles, the tava is hot enough. Wipe off the water with a kitchen towel, and reduce the heat.
7. Pour a ladleful of the batter over the tava. Spread the batter quickly, in a continuous spiral movement, until the Pesarettu is about 12-15 cm in diameter.
8. Drizzle a teaspoon of oil around the edges. Increase the heat and cook for 2-3 minutes, until the base of the Pesarettu is lightly browned. Flip over and cook the other side for another 2-3 minutes, until crisp and golden in color.
9. Transfer to a serving dish. Place a tablespoon of the Onion Topping on it and spread it slightly. Serve hot with Coconut Chutney or Tomato Chutney.

Memo : Pesarettu is easier to make than the traditional dosa. The batter can be used immediately, without fermenting.
The Pesarettu tastes better, if the batter is fermented for 4-6 hours.
The Batter can be kept for 3-4 days in the refrigerator for later use.

Tiffin

Uppama

Savory Semolina　ウプマ（セモリナ小麦炒め）

味わい豊かなセモリナ粉を使用し、玉ねぎとスパイス、カレーリーフで味つけしたヘルシーな朝食。
A wholesome breakfast dish seasoned with onions, spices and curry leaves.

材料　4人分
セモリナ粉　1カップ
お好みの油　大さじ1
カシューナッツ　5〜7粒（砕く）
玉ねぎ　1個（みじん）
生姜　小さじ1（みじん）
青唐辛子　1本（みじん）
塩　適量
コリアンダーリーフ　適量
ココナッツシュレッド　適量
テンパリング
ギー　大さじ1
マスタードシード　小さじ1
鷹の爪　1本
チャナ豆　大さじ1
ウラド豆　大さじ1
カレーリーフ　6〜8枚

1 鍋に水2・1/2カップを入れて沸騰させる。
2 フライパンにセモリナ粉を入れ、茶色くなるまで中火で炒る。
3 大きな鍋に油を入れ加熱し、カシューナッツをきつね色になるまで1〜2分間炒めたら取り出す。
4 テンパリングをする。3のフライパンにギーを入れ加熱し、材料を入れパチパチとはじけ豆の色が変わるまでかき混ぜながら炒める。
5 さらに玉ねぎ、生姜、青唐辛子を入れ、玉ねぎが半透明になるまで中火で2〜3分間炒める。
6 2と塩を加え、1を少量ずつ加える。セモリナ粉が水分を吸い込むまで、かき混ぜながら中火で2〜3分間加熱し、さらにフタをして2〜3分加熱する。
7 3を加えてよく混ぜ、コリアンダーリーフとココナッツシュレッドをトッピングする。ココナッツチャツネやサンバルと一緒に食べる。

バリエーション：工程5で人参、インゲン豆、グリーンピースを合わせてカップ1を入れるとベジタブルウプマができます。レーズンを加えても美味しくなります。

Serves 4

1 cup semolina

1 tablespoon oil

5-7 cashews, broken

1 onion, chopped

1 teaspoon ginger, finely chopped

1 green chili, finely chopped

salt to taste

coriander leaves or shredd coconut to garnish

Tempering

1 tablespoon ghee

1 teaspoon mustard seeds

1 teaspoon chana dal

1 teaspoon urad dal

1 dried red chili

6-8 curry leaves

1. In a saucepan, bring 2-1/2 cups water to a boil and set aside.
2. In another saucepan, dry roast the semolina over medium heat, until it turns light brown. Remove from heat and set aside.
3. Heat 1 tablespoon oil in a saucepan, and saute the cashews for 1-2 minutes, until golden brown. Remove with a slotted spoon and set aside.
4. Prepare the Tempering. To the same saucepan, add 1 tablespoon ghee and and mustard seeds, urad dal, chana dal, dried red chili and curry leaves. Stir briefly until the mustard seeds to splutter and the dals to change color.
5. Add the chopped onions, dried red chili, ginger, green chilies and saute for 2-3 minutes over medium heat until the onions turn translucent.
6. Add the roasted semolina and stir to mix. Gradually add the hot water to the semolina. Add salt to taste. Keep stirring over medium heat for 2-3 minutes, until the water is almost absorbed by the semolina. Cover and cook for 2-3 minutes on medium heat
7. Add the sauteed cashews and mix gently. Garnish with coriander leaves and shredded coconut. Serve hot with Coconut Chutney and Onion Sambar.

Variation : For Vegetable Uppama. Add 1 cup of chopped vegetables - carrot, beans, green peas to the onions. Proceed as above. Golden raisins can also be used as a garnish.

Vengaya Oothappam

Rice and Lentil Pancakes with Onion オッタパム（インド風お好み焼き）

ドーサ生地を厚く焼き、細かく切った野菜を色とりどりにふりかけて焼いた軽食。
Oothappam is a thicker version of the traditional dosa topped with chopped vegetables.

材料　15〜20枚
基本の生地（P99）
塩　適量
お好みの油　適宜
玉ねぎ　2個（みじん）
トマト　2個（みじん）
青唐辛子　4本（みじん）
コリアンダーリーフ　適量（みじん）

1 基本の生地をボウルに用意し、塩を混ぜる。
2 平たいフライパンに油を入れ、中火で加熱する。
3 丸いおたまで生地をすくい、フライパンの中央に注ぐ。おたまの底で中心から円を描き、直径8〜10cmに広げる。
4 生地の上に玉ねぎ、トマト、青唐辛子、コリアンダーリーフを振りかける。
5 生地のまわりに少量の油をたらし、2〜3分後ひっくり返し、中火で両面がきつね色になるまで焼く。ココナッツチャツネやトマトチャツネ、熱くしたサンバルと一緒に食べる。

バリエーション：4の工程で、みじん切りにした玉ねぎ、ピーマン、青唐辛子、人参、じゃがいも、チーズなどをふりかけると美味しくなります。

Makes 15-20
1 recipe of Idli and dosa batter (P99)
salt to taste
2 medium onions, finely chopped
2 tomatoes, finely chopped
4 green chilies, finely chopped
coriander leaves, finely chopped
oil to drizzle

1 Prepare the batter as per instructions mentioned on P99. Place a portion of the batter in a bowl. The batter must be of a thick pouring consistency. Add salt to taste and set aside.
2 Heat a nonstick frying pan or tava over medium heat. Grease with 1 teaspoon oil.
3 Pour a heaped ladleful of the dosa batter in the middle of the tava, and spread it like a thick pancake of about 8-10 cm in diameter.
4 Sprinkle some of the finely chopped onions, tomatoes, chilies and coriander on it. Gentry dab on the vegetables.
5 Drizzle 1/2 teaspoon of oil around the Oothappam, let it cook on medium heat. After about 2-3 minutes, turn the Oothappam carefully to the other side, and cook further 2-3 minutes, until golden brown on both sides.
6 Serve hot with Coconut Chutney or Tomato Chutney and Sambar.

Variation : Optional Toppings: onion and green pepper, onions and green chilies, grated carrots, grated cheese, onion and green chilies, finely chopped

---

Home Remedy

Jal Jeera -Cumin Water- クミンウォーター

代謝や消化の促進などに効果があると言われているクミンシードのドリンク。
デトックスにもおすすめです。

Cumin seeds have many health benefits. They are known to speed up metabolism, and aid in digestion. Jal Jeera serves as a great detox drink.

材料　2杯分
クミンシード　小さじ1
はちみつ　小さじ2

鍋に水3カップを入れ、クミンシードを加えて沸騰させる。中火で6〜8分間煮たら、火をとめてクミンシードを濾して除去する。グラスに注ぎ、ハチミツを加えてよくかき混ぜる。

Makes 2 cup
1 teaspoon cumin seeds
2 teaspoon honey

In a saucepan, place 3 cups water. Add the cumin seeds and bring to a boil. Allow to simmer on medium heat for 6-8 minutes. Strain the boiled cumin water, and discard the cumin seeds. Pour into individual glasses. Add honey and stir. Serve at room temperature.

Drink and Dessert

ドリンク＆デザート

食事中や食後に飲みたい甘さひかえめのドリンクをはじめ、夏のほてりをクールダウンしてくれるレモネード、ミルキーでスイートなヨーグルトドリンクなど、南インドを象徴するドリンクレシピをご紹介します。そして、大人から子どもまで大好きなデザートは、食後やおやつに食べたい冷たいムースや、ゴマやピーナッツ、セモリナ小麦を使用した南インドの定番レシピをご紹介。癒しの時間を提供する、どんな場面でも美味しいレシピです。

Masala Mor

Spiced Buttermilk Drink　マサラモル（スパイスバターミルクドリンク）

ヨーグルトドリンクを青唐辛子と生姜などでスパイシーに味つけしたドリンク。
A spicy version of salted buttermilk, flavored with fresh herbs, green chilies and ginger.

材料4人分
ヨーグルト　2・1/2カップ
青唐辛子　1本
生姜　2枚（スライス）
岩塩　小さじ1/4
コリアンダーリーフ　大さじ1（みじん）
テンパリング
ギー　小さじ1
クミンシード　小さじ1/2
カレーリーフ　3〜5枚（みじん）

1　ヨーグルトと水1・1/2カップをブレンダーに入れてなめらかになるまで撹拌する。ピッチャーに入れ替える。
2　青唐辛子と生姜を一緒にすりつぶしたものを、1に加える。30分ほど置きザルで濾して取り出す。
3　岩塩とコリアンダーリーフを加え、よく混ぜる。
4　テンパリングをする。フライパンにギーを入れ加熱し、材料を炒める。3に注ぎよくかき混ぜる。冷蔵庫に入れて冷やして飲む。

Serves 4
3 cups plain yogurt
1 green chili
2 small slices of ginger
1/4 teaspoon rock salt or salt to taste
1 tablespoon fresh coriander leaves, chopped
Tempering
1 teaspoon ghee
1/2 teaspoon cumin seeds
3-5 curry leaves, chopped

1　Place the yogurt in an electric mixer. Add 1・1/2 cup water and blend until smooth. Transfer to a pitcher and set aside.
2　Lightly crush the ginger and chilies together, using a mortar and pestle, and add to the yogurt mix. Let it stand for 30 minutes. Strain the yogurt mixture into a bowl.
3　Add the rock salt, fresh coriander and stir.
4　Prepare the Tempering. Heat 1 teaspoon ghee in a skillet, add the cumin seeds, curry leaves and let them sizzle. Pour over the yogurt drink and mix well. Place in the refrigerator to cool. Serve chilled.

Mor

Buttermilk Drink　モル（バターミルクドリンク）

夏に最適な、爽やかな飲み心地のヨーグルトドリンク。
A refreshing and soothing yogurt drink flavored with roasted cumin, ideal for Summer.

材料　4人分
ヨーグルト　3カップ
塩　適量
クミンシード　小さじ1/2（すりつぶす）

1　ヨーグルト、塩、水1・1/2カップをブレンダーに入れ、なめらかになるまで混ぜ合わせる。
2　クミンシードを加え、冷蔵庫で冷やして飲む。

Serves 4
3 cups plain yogurt
1/2 teaspoon cumin seeds, roasted and ground
salt to taste

1　Place the yogurt in an electric mixer. Add 1・1/2 cup water, salt to taste and blend until smooth. Transfer to a pitcher. Pour in individual glasses.
2　Add ground cumin powder and serve chilled.

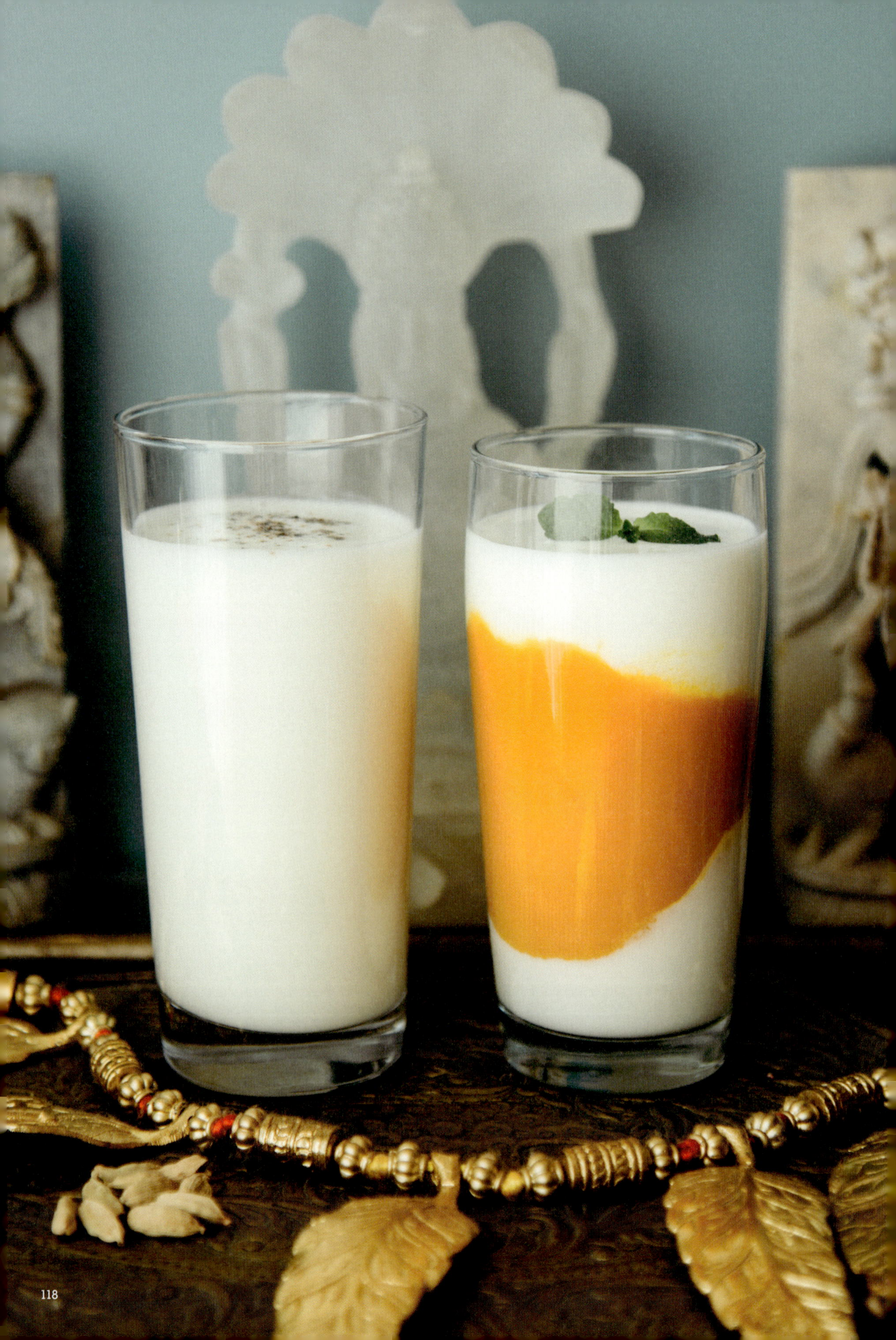

Inippu Tayir

Sweet Yogurt Drink　スイートヨーグルトドリンク

北インドでは「ラッシー」として知られているカルダモン風味の甘いヨーグルトドリンク。
This sweetened yogurt drink flavored with cardamom is also known as Lassi in North India.

材料　4人分
ヨーグルト　3カップ
牛乳　1/4カップ
甘味料　大さじ4
カルダモンパウダー　小さじ1/4

カルダモンパウダー以外の材料と水1カップをブレンダーに入れ、約1分攪拌する。カルダモンパウダーを加えてよく混ぜ、グラスに注ぎ、冷蔵庫で冷やして飲む。

バリエーション：カルダモンラッシーにバナナ2本を加えるとバナナラッシーができます。
カルダモンラッシーにいちご300gを加えるとストロベリーラッシーができます。

Serves 4
3 cups yogurt
1/4 cup milk
4 tablespoon powdered sugar
1/4 teaspoon cardamom powder

1　Place the yogurt and milk in a blender. Add 1 cup water, sugar and process for a minute. Stir in the ground cardamom.
2　Pour the yogurt drink into individual glasses and serve chilled.

Variation：For Banana Yogurt drink. Add 2 bananas to the yogurt and proceed as above. Place all the ingredients in an electric mixer and blend until smooth. Serve chilled.
For Strawberry Yogurt drink. Use 300g fresh or frozen strawberries instead of the banana and proceed as above.

Mambazham Tayir

Mango Yogurt shake　マンゴーヨーグルトシェイク

マンゴー風味のヨーグルトドリンク。完熟マンゴーが理想ですが、缶詰でもOK。
This delicious yogurt drink is like a milkshake. Fresh ripe mangoes are ideal, but canned mango pulp also works.

材料　4人分
完熟マンゴー　1・1/2カップ
ヨーグルト　3カップ
牛乳　1/4カップ
甘味料　大さじ2
ミント　適量

1　ミントの葉以外の材料と水1/4カップをブレンダーに入れ、なめらかになるまで攪拌する。
2　冷蔵庫で冷やし、グラスに注ぎミントを添えて飲む。

Serves 4
1・1/2 cup mango pulp
3 cups yogurt
1/4 cup milk
3 tablespoon sugar
mint leaves to garnish

1　Place the mango pulp, yogurt and milk in a blender. Add 1/4 cup water, sugar and blend until smooth. Place in the refrigerator for an hour
2　Transfer to individual glasses. Top with mint leaves and serve chilled.

Drink
Dessert

Masala Chai

Spiced Tea マサラチャイ

インドではお湯、牛乳、砕いたスパイスと茶葉を合わせて紅茶を作ります。朝食や午後のティータイムに。
In India, tea is brewed by adding tea leaves to a mixture of hot water, milk and crushed whole spices.

材料　2杯分
牛乳　1カップ
アッサム茶葉　大さじ2
甘味料　適量
生姜　1片（つぶす）
ティーマサラ　小さじ1/4

1 鍋に牛乳と水1カップを入れ加熱し、残りの材料を加える。静かにかき混ぜながら、約3〜4分沸騰させる。
2 火からおろし、茶こしなどで濾しながらティーポットに入れ、カップに注ぐ。

Serves 2
1 cup milk
2 teaspoon Assam tea or any black tea
1/4 teaspoon tea masala
a small piece ginger, crushed
2 teaspoon sugar or to taste

1 Place the milk and 1 cup water together in a saucepan. Add the tea leaves, tea masala, crushed ginger and sugar. Bring to a boil and simmer for 3-4 minutes.
2 Remove from heat and strain into a teapot, using a very fine sieve. Pour into individual cups and serve piping hot.

Tea Masala ティーマサラ

材料　1/4カップ分
黒胡椒　大さじ3
カルダモン　大さじ2
生姜パウダー　大さじ2
クローブ　大さじ1/2
シナモンスティック　小1本
ナツメグパウダー　大さじ1/2

すべての材料をブレンダーに入れ、細かくなるまで撹拌する。密閉容器に入れて保存する。

Makes 1/4 cup
3 tablespoon black peppercorn
2 tablespoon cardamom
2 tablespoon dried ginger powder
1/2 tablespoon cloves
1 small stick cinnamon
1/2 tablespoon ground nutmeg

Place all the ingredients in an electric mixer and grind to a smooth powder. Store in an airtight container and use as needed.

Nimboo Pani　Spiced Indian lemonade
インド風レモネード

岩塩と黒胡椒で味つけするインドのレモネード。夏の暑さと渇きをエネルギーに変えてくれます。
This refreshing Indian lemonade flavored with rock salt works as an energy drink in the unrelenting summer heat.

材料　2杯分
レモン汁　大さじ4
甘味料　大さじ8
岩塩　小さじ1/4
黒胡椒　8〜10粒
ミント　適量
レモンスライス　2枚

1 ボウルにレモンスライス以外の材料を入れ、甘味料が
　溶けるまでよく混ぜる。
2 冷水3カップを加え、よく混ぜる。
3 グラスに注ぎ、ミントとレモンスライスを飾る。

メモ：チャトマサラやクミンパウダーを1つまみ加えて、
風味を変えてもOK。

Makes 2 glasses
4 tablespoon lemon juice
1/4 cup sugar
1/4 rock salt or salt to taste
8-10 peppercorns, coarsely ground
Lemon wedges, mint leaves to garnish

1 Squeeze the juice of the lemons in a bowl. Add sugar, rock
　salt, ground pepper, few torn mint leaves, and mix until the
　sugar is dissolved.
2 Add 3 cups iced water and stir to mix. Adjust the sugar and
　salt to taste.
3 Pour into individual glasses. Garnish with lemon wedges, mint
　leaves and serve chilled.

Memo : A pinch of chat masala or ground cumin seeds may be
added for extra flavor.

Drink
Dessert

Filter Coffee Madras Coffee マドラスコーヒー

南インドを代表するコーヒー。鍋で作る方法とインド式コーヒーフィルターを使う方法をご紹介。
Aromatic filter coffee is a signature of South India. Strong, milky and frothy, it is brewed in a special decoction container.

（インスタントの場合）材料　2杯分
牛乳　1・1/2カップ
インスタントコーヒー　小さじ2
甘味料　小さじ2

鍋に牛乳を入れ加熱する。ボウルにインスタントコーヒーと熱湯1/2カップを入れ、カップに注ぎ甘味料を入れる。牛乳を足す。

（コーヒーフィルターの場合）材料　2杯分
フィルター専用コーヒー豆　大さじ2
牛乳　2カップ
甘味料　小さじ2

1 コーヒー豆をフィルターに入れプレスする。
2 熱湯1カップを入れ、10〜15分コーヒーが抽出されるのを待つ。その間に鍋に牛乳を入れて温める。
3 カップに2のコーヒーを入れ、温めた牛乳を注ぐ。
4 甘味料を加えて飲む。

Filter Coffee in a Saucepan : Serves 2
1·1/2 cup milk
1/2 cup water
3 teaspoon instant premium coffee powder
2 teaspoon sugar or to taste

1 In a saucepan, place the milk and bring to a boil. Set aside.
2 In a bowl, dissolve 3 teaspoon coffee powder in 1/2 cup of hot water. Add to the hot milk, and bring to a boil.
3 Pour the coffee in individual cups. Add sugar, and stir to mix. Serve immediately.

Filter Coffee in Decoction Container : Serves 2
2 tablespoon filter coffee powder
1 cup water
2 cups milk
2 teaspoon sugar, or to taste

1 Assemble the container. Place the filter coffee powder in the upper compartment and press lightly with the presser.
2 Bring 1 cup water to a boil, and pour over the coffee powder. Cover the lid and allow the water to seep into the lower compartment. It may take 10-15 minutes to percolate completely. This percolated liquid is the coffee decoction.
3 Heat the milk in a saucepan. Remove from heat and set aside.
4 Place 1 tablespoon of the decoction in individual cups. Pour hot milk over it. Add sugar and stir to mix. Serve hot.

Drink
Dessert

Ellu Urundai

Sesame Laddoo セサミラドゥー（カリカリごま団子）

黒糖を使用した南インドで人気のゴマのお菓子。

Sesame seeds mixed with jaggery. Laddoo is a popular sweet in South India.

材料　20〜24個分

白ゴマ　350g

ピーナッツ　150g

黒糖　300g

1 平たい大きめのフライパンにゴマを入れ、色が変わるまで3〜4分中火で炒り、とり出しておく。

2 1のフライパンで、ピーナッツを3〜4分炒る。うっすらと色が変わったら火からおろし、粗熱がとれたら粗めに砕きゴマと一緒にしておく。

3 鍋に黒糖を入れ加熱して溶かす。ふつふつと泡が立ってきたら火力を弱めて、2を加える。

4 火からおろして全体をよく混ぜ合わせる。

5 平皿に移し、熱いうちに手にとって一口サイズのボール状に成型する。冷めたら密閉容器で保存する。

メモ：熱いうちに成型することで、きれいな丸いかたちになります。

ピーナッツを使用しない場合は、500gの白ゴマと300gの黒糖を使用します。

Makes 20-24

350g white sesame seeds

300g jaggery, powdered

150g peanuts

1 Heat a broad base saucepan, dry roast the sesame seeds lightly over medium heat for 2-3 minutes, stirring continuously until the seeds change color. Remove from heat and set aside.

2 In the same saucepan, dry roast the peanuts for 3-4 minutes, stirring constantly until lightly browned. Cool and rub with the fingers to remove the skin. Crush coarsely and set aside.

3 Heat a non-stick saucepan, place the jaggery, and allow it to melt. When the mixture gets frothy, reduce the heat and quickly add the peanuts and the sesame seeds.

4 Remove from heat and mix thoroughly. Transfer to a bowl and shape the mixture into tiny balls while still hot.

5 Allow the sesame Laddoo to cool. Store in an air-tight container.

Memo：The mixture will harden as it cools, so it is important to shape the Laddoos, immediately, while the mixture is still hot.

If using only sesame seeds, use 500g sesame seeds and 300g jaggery. Proceed as above.

—————— Home Remedy ——————

風邪をひいたときに

For relief from common cold

Ginger and Jaggery Balls

生姜と黒糖のお団子

生姜パウダー　大さじ1

黒糖　大さじ1

ハチミツ　小さじ1

混ぜて小さく丸め、1日に何度か食べましょう。

1 tablespoon dried ginger powder

1 tablespoon powdered jaggery

1 teaspoon honey

Mix and divide into tiny balls and have over the day.

Verkadalai Chikki

Peanut Brittle ピーナッツタフィー

子どもから大人まで皆に愛される、ピーナッツとキャラメリゼのスイーツ。
A delicious sweet of caramelized peanuts that is popular with children and adults alike.

材料　12〜14枚
ピーナッツ　1カップ
ギー　適宜
黒糖　1カップ

1 平たい大きめのフライパンにピーナッツを入れ、3〜4分中火で炒り、とり出して粗熱をとる。指で皮をむいてから、粗めに砕く。
2 平皿と麺棒にギーを塗っておく。
3 フライパンにギー大さじ1を入れ加熱し、黒糖を加えて中火で溶かす。2〜3分軽く沸騰させたら弱火にして1分加熱する。
4 火からおろし、すぐにピーナッツを加えて木べらでよく混ぜる。
5 平皿に流し入れ、ギーをつけた麺棒を使って2〜3mmの薄く均一な厚さに広げる。熱いうちに包丁で正方形に切り分けて冷ます。密閉容器で保存する。
6 そのままおやつとして、または茶菓子として食べる。

メモ：ピーナッツを入れた生地は、冷めるにつれ固くなるので、熱いうちに流し入れ包丁でカットするのがポイント。

Makes 12-14 pieces
1 · 1/2 cups raw peanuts
1tablespoon ghee
1 cup jaggery
ghee for greasing

1 Heat a saucepan, and dry roast the peanuts over medium heat for 3-4 minutes, stirring constantly until lightly browned. Remove from heat and set aside to cool. Rub with your fingers to remove the skin. Coarsely grind the roasted peanuts and set aside.
2 Grease a rolling pin, and a counter top or a flat dish with ghee, and keep ready.
3 Heat the non-stick saucepan on medium heat. Add the ghee and jaggery and keep stirring for 2-3 minutes, until the jaggery dissolves. Allow to simmer on low heat for a minute.
4 When the jaggery gets frothy, remove from heat, add the crushed peanuts and mix thoroughly.
5 Pour onto the greased flat dish and quickly roll the mixture flat, using the greased rolling pin.
6 Cut into small squares using a knife, while still hot. Allow the mixture to cool. Break it into small pieces and store in an air tight container. Serve as a snack or as a sweet treat with tea.

Memo：The mixture will harden as it cools, so it is important to make the desired cuts into the peanut mixture while it is still hot.

Shrikhand

Sweet Yogurt with Cardamom ヨーグルトムース

グジャラート州ならではのカルダモンとヨーグルトのデザート。

A sweet dish from my native region of Gujarat, Shrikhand is a popular dessert across India, usually served as part of a meal.

材料　4人分

ヨーグルト　500g

粉糖　3/4カップ

カルダモンパウダー　小さじ1/4

アーモンド　6〜8個（スライス）

ピスタチオ　6〜8個（スライス）

1 ヨーグルトを木綿布やキッチンペーパーなどで1〜2時間水切りする。
2 ボウルに1と粉糖を入れてよく混ぜたら、濾してカルダモンパウダーを加えて混ぜる。
3 アーモンドとピスタチオを添える。

Serves 4

500g Greek yogurt or regular yogurt

3/4 cup powdered sugar

1/4 teaspoon cardamom powder

6-8 pistachios, slivered

6-8 almonds, slivered

1 Place the yogurt in a muslin cloth. Let the excess liquid drain for about 1-2 hours. The yogurt will get slightly firm and creamy.
2 Transfer the hung yogurt to a bowl. Add sugar and mix. Pass the mixture through a fine sieve and set aside. Add cardamom powder and mix. Transfer to a serving bowl.
3 Garnish with almond and pistachios. Serve chilled.

Mambazham Shrikhand

Mango Yogurt マンゴーヨーグルトムース

マンゴーのフルーティーでエキゾチックな味わいと香りが人気のデザート。

A richer variation of the classic Shrikhand. Fresh mango lends an exotic flavor to this popular summer dessert.

材料　4人分

ヨーグルト　500g
生クリーム　1/2カップ
粉糖　3/4カップ
マンゴーピューレ　1カップ
マンゴー　適量（角切り）
ミント　適量

1　ヨーグルトを木綿布やキッチンペーパーなどで1〜2時間水切りする。
2　ボウルに生クリームを入れ、ハンドミキサーで泡立て、1を加えて混ぜる。
3　粉糖を加えて溶かし、マンゴーピューレを加えて全体をよく混ぜる。
4　器に盛りマンゴーとミントをトッピングする。

Serves 4

500g Greek yogurt or regular yogurt
3/4 cup powdered sugar
1/2 cup fresh cream
1 cup mango pulp
fresh mango and mint leaves to garnish

1　Place the yogurt in a muslin cloth. Let the excess liquid drain for about 1-2 hours, until the yogurt will get slightly firm and creamy. Transfer to a bowl and mix until smooth.
2　In another bowl, whisk the fresh cream for 5-6 minutes, until it thickens slightly.
3　Add the whisked cream, powdered sugar and mango pulp to the drained yogurt and mix thoroughly.
4　Transfer to a serving bowl and refrigerate for 2-3 hours. Garnish with sliced mango and fresh mint leaves. Serve chilled.

Drink
Dessert

Rava Kesari

Semolina Pudding セモリナプディング

ローストしたセモリナ粉を使用したコクのある味わいのデザート。

Lightly-roasted semolina infused with aromatic cardamom and saffron, topped with raisins and cashews.

材料　4人分

ギー　大さじ4

カシューナッツ　大さじ1

レーズン　10〜15粒

セモリナ小麦　1カップ

A
| 牛乳　1・1/2カップ
| 甘味料　1カップ
| カルダモンパウダー　小さじ1/2
| サフラン　1つまみ

1 フライパンにギー大さじ1を入れて加熱する。カシューナッツを加え、きつね色になったらレーズンを加えて軽く炒め、カシューナッツとレーズンをとり出しておく。

2 1のフライパンに残りのギーを入れ、セモリナ小麦を加えて色がうっすら変わり、香りが出るまで3〜4分炒める。

3 鍋にAと水1カップを入れ加熱し、一度沸騰させてから2〜3分弱火にして加熱する。

4 2に3を加えて、4〜5分よくかき混ぜる。油分が分離してフライパンの周りに浮いてくるまでが目安。

5 1を加え、よく混ぜ合わせたら器に盛り、サフランを飾る。温かいうちに食べる。

メモ：アーモンドスライスをトッピングすると、より美味しくなります。

Serves 4

4 tablespoon ghee

1 tablespoon cashews

1 cup semolina (cream of wheat)

1・1/2 cup milk

1 cup sugar

10-15 raisins

1/2 teaspoon cardamom powder

few strands of saffron

1 Heat 1 tablespoon of the ghee in a non-stick pan and saute the cashews, on medium heat, until golden. Add raisins and stir. Remove the cashews and raisins with a slotted spoon and set aside.

2 Add the remaining 3 tablespoons ghee to the pan, and stir- fry the semolina for 3-4 minutes over medium heat, until lightly colored and fragrant. Set aside.

3 In another saucepan, combine the milk with 1 cup water and bring to a boil. Add the saffron strands, sugar and cardamom powder. Simmer for 2-3 minutes until the sugar dissolves. Remove from heat.

4 To Finish. Heat the saucepan with the semolina. Gradually add the milk and water mixture to the semolina, and keep stirring for 4-5 minutes over medium heat, until the liquid is absorbed and the ghee is visible on the sides. Remove from heat and keep covered and for 2-3 minutes.

5 Transfer to a serving dish. Garnish with the sauteed cashews, raisins and serve hot.

Memo : 6-8 almonds, slivered may be used as an optional garnish.

Paal Payasam

Flavored Sweetened Milk　パールパイサム（ライスプディング）

サフランとカルダモンを使用した、結婚式やお祭りなどで人気のクリーミーなデザート。
This rich and creamy dessert, flavored with saffron and cardamom, is served at festivals and on auspicious occasions.

材料　4人分

長粒米　1/4カップ
牛乳　8カップ
お好みの甘味料　1/2カップ〜
アーモンド　8〜10個（スライス）
カルダモンパウダー　小さじ1
サフラン　適宜

1　30分浸水した長粒米を少量の水とブレンダーに入れ、粒が残る程度に撹拌し、ボウルに移す。
2　厚めの鍋に牛乳を入れ、沸騰させる。1を加え、かき混ぜながらしばらく中火で加熱する。
3　鍋の底に、ペーストの塊ができないよう木べらを使用して時々かき混ぜる。25〜30分加熱する。
4　長粒米に火が通ったら甘味料、アーモンド、カルダモンパウダーを加える。
5　甘味料が溶けるまで3〜4分煮る。器に盛り、サフランをトッピングする。お好みで温かいまま、もしくは冷たくして食べる。

バリエーション：人参2本をすりおろして長粒米の代わりに使用すると、人参パイサムができます。甘味料と一緒にアーモンドパウダーを大さじ2加えるとより濃厚になります。ギー大さじ1にカシューナッツ大さじ2、レーズン大さじ1、ココナッツパウダー大さじ2を炒め、できあがったパイサムにトッピングするのもおすすめ。

Serves 4

1/4 cup long grain rice
8 cups milk
1/2 cup sugar(more if desired)
8-10 almonds, sliced
1/2 teaspoon cardamom powder
1/2 teaspoon saffron strands- optional
few saffron strands for garnish

1　Soak the rice in 1 cup water for 30 minutes. Drain and place in an electric mixer. Grind to a coarse paste, using a little water. The rice should still feel grainy. Transfer to a bowl and set aside.
2　Place the milk in a heavy saucepan and bring to a boil. Add the coarsely ground rice paste and keep stirring for a while, over medium heat.
3　Simmer for 25-30 minutes, stirring occasionally so that the rice does not settle onto the base as a lump. When the rice is cooked and mixture has thickened a bit, add the sugar, almonds, and cardamom powder.
4　Simmer for 3-4 minutes, until the sugar has dissolved. Transter to a serving bowl.
5　Garnish with saffron strands and serve. Payasam can be served hot or chilled.

Variation : For Carrot Payasam, Add 2 carrots, peeled and grated to the milk, instead of the rice. Add 2 tablespoon of powdered almonds with the sugar for a richer flavor. Proceed to cook as above.
Paal payasam will thicken when it cools or after refrigeration. You may add a little milk to it before serving to make it thinner.

Recomended Shops

インド料理におすすめのお店

Ambika masala shop

アンビカ マサラ ショップ

チリパウダーホット
Chilly Powder Hot

100g ¥240＋tax

コリアンダーパウダー
Coriander Powder

100g ¥240＋tax

クミンパウダー
Cumin Powder

100g ¥270＋tax

ターメリックパウダー
Turmeric Powder

100g ¥260＋tax

ココナッツトレード
Coconut Thread

100g ¥240＋tax

グリーンカルダモンパウダー
Green Cardamom Powder

50g ¥390＋tax

シナモンスティック
Cinnamon Stick

50g ¥240＋tax

コリアンダーホール
Coriander Whole

50g ¥240＋tax

Information

高品質なインド産のスパイス・ハーブ・調味料・米などをはじめ、インド料理に欠かせない専門食材やスナック、フルーツジュースを輸入・開発・販売。日本語、ヒンドゥー語、英語対応。

Importing and selling high quality spices, herbs, seasonings, rice and other specialty food from India including snacks and fruit juices. Japanese, Hindi and English friendly store.

東京都台東区蔵前 3-19-2 アンビカハウス
3-19-2, Kuramae, Taito-ku, Tokyo
TEL : 03-6908-8077

shop@ambikajapan.com
ambikajapan.com

Alishan
アリサン

有機ひよこ豆
Organic Chana Dal
⊕
500g ¥600＋tax

有機ムング豆
Organic Mung Dal
⊕
500g ¥650＋tax

有機レンズ豆
Organic Rentil Dal
⊕
500g ¥690＋tax

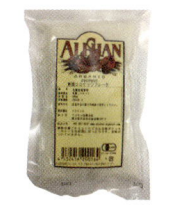 

クミンシード
Cumin Seed
⊕
20g ¥420＋tax

有機ココナッツフレーク
Organic Coconut Flake
⊕
100g ¥220＋tax

有機ココナッツオイル
Organic Coconut Oil
⊕
300g ¥1,000＋tax

Information

世界十数カ国から、オーガニック＆ベジタリアンフードを輸入し、卸売り及び個人通販を行う。社屋のある緑豊かな埼玉県日高市では、自社輸入食材と地元農家の有機野菜をふんだんに使った阿里山カフェを運営。

Importing and retailing Organic & Vegetarian food from all over the world.
Local fresh and organic vegetables are used along with the imported ingredients at the Alishan Café located in Hidaka, Saitama.

埼玉県日高市高麗本郷 185-2
185-2, Komahongoh, hidaka-shi, Saitama
TEL：0429-82-4811
alishan-organics.com

阿里山カフェ
TEL：0429-82-4823

Online Shop store.alishan.jp/ja

マスコットフーズ株式会社

マスタードシード（ブラウン）
Mustard Seed（Brown）
⊕
45g ¥380＋tax

ターメリック
Turmeric
⊕
30g ¥280＋tax

カイエンヌペッパー
Cayenne Pepper
⊕
25g ¥280＋tax

  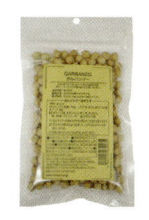

クミンシード
Cumin Seed
⊕
30g ¥330＋tax

コリアンダーシードパウダー
Coriander Seed Powder
⊕
22g ¥330＋tax

ガルバンゾー
Garbanzo
⊕
200g ¥330＋tax

Information

スパイス専門メーカー。定番のスパイス、ハーブをはじめ、オリジナルシーズニングやハーブ、スパイスミックスなど、選りすぐりのラインナップで「世界の香りとおいしさ」をご家庭のキッチンにお届け。

Delivering "The flavors and fragrances of spices from the world"
Mascot foods is a traditional spice company. You can find selections of classic spices, herbs, original seasonings and other spice mixes.

東京都品川区西五反田 5-23-2
5-23-2, Nishi-gotanda,
Shinagawa-ku, Tokyo
TEL：03-3490-8418

shop.mascot.co.jp

おわりに

　無条件の愛とサポートをあたえ、私のお手本になってくれている父ラルチャンド・ガンディーと母ニラ・ガンディー。私の人生の大きな癒しとなっている妹のカルパナ、シパ、リナ。そして大きな大黒柱である弟のケタン。私の最も素晴らしいファンであり、最も辛辣な意見をくれた娘のアイーシャと息子のアロック。私のことを信じ、夜遅い編集作業の間も紅茶を入れ続けてくれてありがとう。私の人生の旅に貢献してくれた世界中にいる大切な友人と家族、そして私の夫アトゥル。レシピや料理のテクニックをシェアしてくださった、ダクシナヤン・レストラン経営者のビーナ・ガンディー氏とヘムル・ガンティー氏、オーキッドホテルのサウス・オブ・ヴィンディアス・レストランのマスターシェフ、バラ・スブラマニアム氏とエグゼクティブシェフのナヴィッド・サイド氏、マドラスカフェのデヴァヴラット・カマス氏、プレマ・シェティ氏とプシュカラ・マニ氏にも心からお礼を申し上げます。この本を制作するにあたり、皆さんからのご指導は計り知れないほど貴重なものでした。

　温かいコーヒーとともに、場所と時間を提供してくれたシューバ・アイヤル氏。

　制作中、いつも電話でフォローと励ましをくれたディリー・ダバ氏、ロクサラ・ダバ氏、プリシー・ラオ・パテル氏、ビーナ・ガンディ氏、シュバ・アイヤー氏。そして、私の言葉の中にある気持ちを翻訳してくださった鈴木里英氏、原木洋子氏。

　また、アンビカ・トレーディング・カンパニーの社長のニティン・ヒンガル氏のパートナーシップとサポートに感謝します。アンビカ・ジャパン提供のスパイスや新鮮な材料のおかげで、この本でご覧いただけるレシピの風味と色は豊かになりました。

　私を支え、励ましてくださった制作チーム（編集の渡邉氏、カメラマンの宗野氏、デザイナーの松本氏）。皆さんと一緒に制作できたことは大きな喜びです。

　最後に、この本のビジョンに賛同し出版をしてくださったキラジェンヌ株式会社の代表・吉良さおりさん。心から感謝の気持ちを捧げます。

Acknowledgements

I would like to extend my heartfelt gratitude and appreciation to

My father, Lalchand Gandhi and my mother, Nila Gandhi for their unconditional love and support.

My sisters, Kalpana, Shilpa and Rina, for being the calming force in my life.

My brother Ketan, for being a pillar of strength to me.

My children Ayesha and Alok, for being my greatest fans and most honest critics. Thank you for believing in me and for the long nights of edits with endless cups of tea.

My husband Atul, and my cherished friends and family all over the world. Each one of you has contributed to my life journey.

Hemul and Beena Gandhi, Proprietor of Dakhinayan restaurant, Mumbai and Ahmedabad, Master Chef Bala Subramanium and Executive Chef Navid Sayyed of South Of Vindyas restaurant, Mumbai, Devavrat Kamath of Madras Café, Mumbai, Prema Shetty, and Pushkala Mani, for sharing their homes, recipes and cooking techniques with me. Their expertise and guidance was invaluable in my research for this book.

Shubha Iyer for generously sharing her home and time with me. Thank you for the hours spent together, reviewing my recipes over hot cups of coffee.

Dilly Daver, Roxana Daver, Preethy Rao Patel, Beena, Shubha and Rie, for their continuous encouragement throughout the writing of this book. Thank you for always being just a phone call away.

Rie Suzuki and Yoko Haraki for their generous help with the Japanese translation of my story. Together, they have beautifully expressed the feelings behind my words.

Nitin Hingarh, President, Ambika Trading Co, for his partnership and support. The spices and ingredients from Ambika, Japan have enriched the flavors and colors of the recipes in this book.

The Kirasienne team, editor Eriko Watanabe, Photographer Ayumu Muneno, Designer Nami Matsumoto, for their support and encouragement. It was indeed a pleasure to work with all of you.

Lastly, a special thank you to Saori Kira of KIRASIENNE Inc, whose confidence and vision made this book possible.

Hema Parekh
ヘーマ・パレック

インド＆アジアのベジタリアン料理専門家。ハーブやスパイスの魔法を使い、新鮮な食材で栄養価の高いさまざまな料理を研究し生み出しながら、25年以上に渡り料理講師、栄養士、料理コンサルタントとして、幅広く活動している。著書は『インド式菜食生活』（グラフ社）、『Asian Vegan Kitchen（英文版）』（講談社インターナショナル）ほか。

Hema Parekh specializes in Indian and Asian vegetarian cooking, and is dedicated to nutritious, authentic dining using fresh ingredients with the magic of herbs and spices. The author of several cookbooks including The Asian Vegan Kitchen, Hema has been a certified teacher, nutritionist and culinary consultant in Japan for over 25 years.

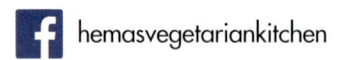 hemasvegetariankitchen

撮影／宗野 歩

編集・校正／渡邉 絵梨子

デザイン／株式会社 ACQUA

THE
South Indian
Vegetarian Kitchen
はじめてのベジタリアン南インド料理

Hema Parekh
ヘーマ・パレック

2017 年 11 月 30 日　初版発行

発行人　吉良さおり

発行所　キラジェンヌ株式会社

〒 151-0073　東京都渋谷区笹塚 3-10-2 青田ビル 2F

TEL：03-5371-0041

http://www.kirasienne.com

印刷・製本　モリモト印刷株式会社